GODLY
SORROW
WORKS

David J. Smith

GODLY SORROW WORKS

SEVEN EVIDENCES OF A MATURING LIFE IN CHRIST

CLC ✦ PUBLICATIONS
Fort Washington, PA 19034

Published by CLC ❖ Publications

U.S.A.
P.O. Box 1449, Fort Washington, PA 19034

GREAT BRITAIN
51 The Dean, Alresford, Hants. SO24 9BJ

AUSTRALIA
P.O. Box 419M, Manunda, QLD 4879

NEW ZEALAND
10 MacArthur Street, Feilding

ISBN 0-87508-775-2

Copyright © 2002
David J. Smith

This printing 2003

Printed in the United States of America

This book is dedicated to
Dr. Dennis F. Kinlaw, who was
President of Asbury College when
I attended as a new Christian.
He taught the highest scriptural standards
and lived by them, helping instill
in me the desire to do the same.

Contents

Abbreviations

AMP: The Amplified Bible (1954)
ASV: American Standard Version (1901)
CEV: Contemporary English Version (1991)
KJV: King James Version (1611)
NASB: New American Standard Bible (1960)
NEB: New English Bible (1961)
NIV: New International Version (1973)
NKJV: New King James Version (1982)
NLT: New Living Translation (1996)
RSV: Revised Standard Version (1946)
TEV: Today's English Version (1966)
TLB: The Living Bible (1971)

. . . . .

Beck: The New Testament in the Language of Today (1963)
The Message (1993)
Phillips: The New Testament by J.B. Phillips (1957)
Williams: The New Testament in the Language of the People (1937)

Introduction

I was talking with Nene (pronounced NEH-neh), a young mother from one of the numerous pagan tribes of Guinea-Bissau. She was recounting how she had been converted about three years earlier. When she received Jesus, her father was furious. She was young, about 14 years old. (That was a guess, because like many, her birth had never been registered.) She was pretty. She was a virgin. This meant she was extremely marketable and would fetch a very good bride price. However, the men of the tribe would not want to marry a believer in Jesus: she would certainly bring the wrath of their tribal deities upon any household to which she belonged. She could even be responsible for disease or disaster which might come upon an entire village.

Her father could not persuade her to renounce her new faith, so he tried force. Every day he took her outside and beat her violently. He was not moved to pity by her screams of pain. Every day she was told that if she renounced her faith and returned to worship the tribal idols, the beatings would stop. She refused because she knew Jesus and what He had endured for her.

After a number of weeks her father realized Nene would rather die than deny Jesus. He finally tired of the daily beatings. Amazingly enough, a man was found who was willing to marry her, although he was not willing to pay much. Shortly after the marriage they left their tribal area and moved to the city of Bafata, where Linda and I served as church planters with WEC (Worldwide Evangelization for Christ) International in Guinea-Bissau, a small country in West Africa. We had the joy of helping her grow in her faith for a few weeks until she and her husband and son moved on to the country of Senegal just north of us.

Perhaps five years earlier I was talking to a pastor near Portsmouth, Ohio, where I pastored four small churches. His cheek was distorted due to a large wad of chewing tobacco. He commented that when he went to the altar to be saved he had tobacco in his mouth, and he figured it was still quite acceptable. In fact, giving up chewing tobacco did not even appear negotiable.

Which of the two, Nene or the pastor, was the more responsive to the Spirit of God? I don't blame you if you don't want to answer, since you have only the tiniest bit of information about each one. You have no idea if Nene had sinful habits I haven't mentioned, or if the pastor showed evidence of tremendous transformation in many areas of his life. So while it would be folly for you to make a spiritual evaluation in this case, please notice that the issue of evaluating spiritual life and growth runs through the entire Bible. It is also the topic of this book. Certainly we who name Jesus as our Savior expect personal guidance from the Holy Spirit. This is our *right* as believers. However, such guidance is subjective and very personal, and ultimately is in no way subject to review by others. "This is between God and me." "God is my judge." "Who are you to be another person's conscience?" "Judge not, lest you be judged!" Have you heard any of these? How about, "Take care of the mote, beam, log, or whatever is in your own eye first!"

Just to let you know, I have been on the receiving end of "judgments." During my second year as a Christian I attended Asbury College in Wilmore, Kentucky. I had a job selling Bible reference books door-to-door with the Southwestern Company that summer. I am not a salesman by nature, but God richly blessed me that summer and I earned more than enough to pay for the entire upcoming academic year.

One afternoon I was sitting on the front porch

of the home of a man to whom I had just made my presentation. He did not want the books but showed an interest in conversation, so we just sat and talked for a while. We talked of Jesus and of heaven. Then he asked what church I attended. I wished he hadn't because I already knew he attended a strict association of churches (they don't use the word "denomination") that teach that only those who belong to that association are saved. Still, after the great time we had, I hoped he might be more moderate in his personal belief. When I answered, he looked like he had lost a dear friend and he seemed almost ready to weep, because I was certainly going to hell. He told me how unspeakably sorry he was for me.

On another occasion a couple of years later, while I was a student at Asbury Seminary, I was facing a decision about leaving the four churches I mentioned earlier. As I was driving back to Asbury from Ohio on a Sunday evening, I saw lights on in a church along the way. I decided to stop and talk to the pastor and ask for any insights he might have. He was the only person still at the church. I introduced myself and said I would like to talk with him briefly if possible. His response was somewhat unexpected. He asked how I had been baptized. I assured him it was by immersion. He went on to ask what words had been used, because if I had been baptized with the words "in the name of the Father, and of the

Son, and of the Holy Spirit," I was absolutely lost. Only a baptism with the words "in the name of Jesus" was valid. That conversation was over, because as an unrepentant unbeliever I certainly could not hear from God.

Fortunately these are the worst such experiences I have had. However, like many or all who will read this book, I have had questions about God's will concerning my life in terms of career, marriage, actions, attitudes, and probably a number of other things. So I am writing this book as a seeker who has found something that may be useful to other seekers.

For over thirty years I have been involved in ministry: as a pastor in America, a missionary in Guinea-Bissau, West Africa, and as a missionary "mobilizer" for WEC International. In the latter capacity I have spoken to large and small groups in schools and churches across America. I have also spoken privately with thousands of individuals, discussing their questions about spiritual and practical matters.

Though I cannot reconstruct each of these conversations, I am confident I have been asked a few particular questions hundreds of times. Some of these include . . .

"How can I know the will of God for my life?"

"How can I best serve God in America in my present occupation?"

"What are the primary obstacles to becoming a missionary?"

"What about my parents (or children) if I become a missionary?"

"How do I keep from growing stale spiritually?"

"How do you make disciples of those who come to Jesus?"

"What are some essential elements for my spiritual growth?"

"How do I prepare for and deal with spiritual warfare?"

"How do I evaluate my spiritual walk?"

Several of these questions deal uniquely with missions. Others deal with living a Christ-centered life in general. I like both kinds. The first kind I can often answer from the perspective of an occupation—"doing missions," so to speak. The second kind I deal with as a vocation—the common calling given to everyone who has been born again through the death and resurrection of Jesus. Check the dictionary. One definition of vocation is "occupation." However, most definitions refer to a "calling," a "divine direction," if you will, for our lives. We may change our occupation many times throughout our lifetime. Our vocation does *not* change. We are called to *live for Jesus*.

The idea of vocation implies relation. After all, if we are "called" there is a sense of voice involved in the calling, and a sense of hearing by the recipient. The Divine Person (God) is doing the calling. We who are the redeemed hear, respond, and thereby relate as we embrace our heavenly vocation.

A good relationship is built on a good foundation. This begins with a good biblical understanding of salvation and the changes I can expect in my life as the Holy Spirit takes residence in me. In presenting the path to salvation there are various ways to express the truths of sin, guilt, and judgment. Many people have favorite verses they use almost every time they attempt to lead another to Jesus. I do. Each occasion is geared to the particular individual or group, but I will almost always include five or six favorite verses in my presentation. These verses were key to my own conversion and initial growth.

There are many good programs for early growth. I was privileged to study the "Ten Steps To Basic Christian Maturity" by Campus Crusade for Christ, and to memorize a lot of verses through the Navigators programs. As believers grow in the Lord, they become more and more individualized in their study and activities. That's appropriate.

Where am I going with all this? The last question in the previous cluster is how someone can evaluate his present walk with Christ. What a horribly wonderful or wonderfully horrible question to be asked! They don't want to be told they're obviously okay if they are reading the Bible, praying, attending church, tithing, and witnessing. They know these duties can be done in the energy of the flesh by someone with very little or no spiritual life. They know that just being in Bible School is no assurance of spiritual growth. Some of them may have friends who discovered they really weren't saved even after a couple of years of Bible School. They perhaps know others who are working so hard to stuff their heads that their hearts are starving. This may even describe their own life at the time they ask the question about evaluation.

These are not people who are seeking to cling to a habit or justify an action or an attitude. They are looking for clear direction from the Bible which, although it must be applied subjectively to fit their individual circumstances, still contains broad objective truth on which they can reflect as they study.

When we go back to initial salvation, they can tell me how they know they are saved. They will take me through John 3:16, Romans 3:23 and 6:23, 1 John 1:9, Revelation 3:20, Ephesians 2:8–9, or numerous similar verses, and explain how they came to believe these as general truths and then specifically applied them to their own lives. What they want are verses to apply to ongoing growth as simply as they apply these verses to initial salvation. They don't want them by the thousands, or even by the hundreds. They are looking for a few special verses. Yes, they are aware of the greatest command, that they are to "Love the Lord your God with all your heart and with all your soul and with all your mind" (Matthew 22:37; Deuteronomy 6:5). They also know the second, which is to "Love your neighbor as yourself" (Matthew 22:39; Leviticus 19:18).

Is there any kind of simple answer to the question?—some kind of yardstick, barometer or thermometer to register growth and vitality? Simply asking how someone feels about his relationship to Christ is often flawed, due to the fickleness of many who "feel" whatever their emotions dictate on a given day, or at a given hour. Others have a subjectivity that is measured by activity, often measured in hours spent in various spiritual disciplines from Bible study to church to witnessing. Those who don't have any doubts or questions generally aren't asking. So I'm looking for something to share with those who are.

I did an experiment. I asked over 100 friends—some in ministry and some who are lay Christians—to give me five key verses relating to initial salvation and ten key verses relating to Christian growth. I chose the sample to reflect a variety of ages and both genders. I received 69 responses.

I ultimately came up with one short passage. No, it's not the perfect answer. It's a passage I have studied most of my Christian life and have used as a sermon text numerous times over the last ten to fifteen years. It is a passage that I find myself considering in quiet moments of self-evaluation. It may be somewhat like what is recorded in a conversation between F. B. Meyer, a young pastor who became a well-known British author, and C. T. Studd, founder of WEC. This took place in England in 1885, when C.T. Studd was preparing to go to China as a missionary with the China Inland Mission. Meyer writes:

The visit of Messrs. Stanley Smith and Studd to Melbourne Hall will always mark an epoch in my own life. Before then my Christian life had been spasmodic and fitful: now flaming up with enthusiasm, and then pacing wearily over leagues of grey ashes and cold cinders. I saw that these young men had something which I had not, but which was within them a constant source of rest and strength and joy. And never will I forget a scene at 7 a.m. in the grey mist of a November morning, as daylight was flickering into the bedroom, paling the guttering candles which from a very early hour had been lighting up the pages of Scripture, and revealing the figures of the devoted Bible students, who wore the old cricket or boating blazer of earlier days to render them less sensible to the raw, damp climate. The talk we had then was one of the formative influences of my life.

"You have been up early," I said to Charlie Studd. "Yes," said he, "I got up at four o'clock this morning. Christ always knows when I have had sleep enough, and He wakes me to have a good time with Him." I asked, "What have you been doing this morning?" And he replied, "You know that the Lord says, 'If ye love Me, keep My commandments'; and I was just looking through all the commandments that I could find that the Lord gave, and putting a tick against them if I have kept them, because I do love Him."*

Meyer continues to tell how he asked Studd how to have a similar relationship with Christ. Studd explains about deliberately and totally giving himself to Jesus, which Meyer subsequently did.

C.T. Studd was examining Christ's commandments to see if he was keeping them. It was a self-evaluation that he found helpful. Yes, such an examination could easily become legalistic and spiritually deadening rather than liberating and stimulating. But by keeping *love* as the standard—the goal of his search—Studd knew how to continue in the freedom that Christ gives. This was my goal in looking for a key passage. I wanted something challenging, but something that throbbed in unison with the heartbeat of Jesus—something through which I could joyously call out to God to enlarge my un-

---

* Pages 45–46, *C.T. Studd, Cricketer & Pioneer* by Norman Grubb. Published by CLC Ministries (formerly Christian Literature Crusade).

derstanding, my vision, and my passion. It would also be a passage to rebuke me when I became lethargic or lukewarm.

What is this wonderful passage? Just two short verses, 2 Corinthians 7:10–11. **"For godly sorrow worketh repentance to salvation not to be repented of: but the sorrow of the world worketh death. For behold this selfsame thing, that ye sorrowed after a godly sort, what carefulness it wrought in you, yea, what clearing of yourselves, yea, what indignation, yea, what fear, yea, what vehement desire, yea, what zeal, yea, what revenge! In all things ye have approved yourselves to be clear in this matter."** (KJV)

This passage talks about the changes that Paul noticed in the church at Corinth in response to the harsh letter we call First Corinthians. He uses several words or short phrases that show a continuity and a progression. You never quit doing the first even when you have arrived at the last, which is hopefully soon in your walk with Jesus. I find I can ask myself, "Am I walking well in this area?" If so, I am encouraged, and if not, then I hopefully do something about it very soon. In my own life I have found the earlier words and phrases to be easier and the latter more difficult. This may be merely my personality; for others, any injunction in the list may be easier and any harder.

The reason I offer this passage is that, as I said, I have presented it many times. It is not uncommon for someone to thank me immediately after the message, saying how helpful it was. That happens, thankfully, following many messages. However, this is the one message more than all others combined for which people will later say to me, "I am still applying these verses and they continue to help me." I hope they will help you.

(What you will be reading on these pages is, with some further seasoning, a much expanded version of that half-hour sermon.)

As to the 69 responses I got to my questionnaire—and in most cases I received ten or more verses or passages on Christian growth—not one person used this passage in 2 Corinthians 7. In fact, no one even referred to the chapter. So I don't feel I am adding to volumes and volumes of teaching on a commonly used passage.

I want to investigate this passage with you from several versions of Scripture. In the subsequent chapters I will deal with the words and phrases one at a time, and will show how in my life and in the lives of others I have seen growth as these principles are incorporated into the lives of various individuals. These are examples not of people who let others make their spiritual decisions for them; nor are these people who refuse to discuss or consider areas of their personal lives. These are people who know Jesus and want to know Him *more* and grow *closer* to Him! Yes, of course there is subjectivity in this, but a subjectivity based on the study of the Word of God. The result of this study will, I trust, be spiritual growth and an on-going transformation into the likeness of Jesus.

Our opening chapter contains the text and its context. I am giving you an expanded passage in two versions, followed by the two *key verses* in several others. By my doing it this way, I hope that as we progress you can easily flip back and compare the versions. You will recognize that most of these versions are "translations," while the last two are paraphrases which, while interesting to read, don't really attempt to follow the Greek. I won't refer to them in the subsequent chapters.

The final chapter may seem out of place. But there I want to present other verses that I regularly use when sharing with others about the rudiments of spiritual growth. In Africa we actually used them when teaching salvation. Those coming to Christ had absolutely no background of biblical teaching or spiritual understanding—they only knew that what they saw in the lives of those who had previously come to Christ surpassed any hope offered in their present religion. They knew they were coming to the One God, the Almighty God, the True

God. They were coming with *nothing* to Him who offered *everything*. They were willing to serve Him as they had served the spirits of their previous religion. However, Christianity is not a religion, it is a relationship. Therefore we wanted these men and women to know *God*. Only by truly knowing Him could they come to *love* Him. Loving leads to more *knowing*, which leads to more *loving*! The spiral continues upward until finally they meet Him face-to-face as they step from time into eternity.

So it is in my relationship. If I do not keep my focus on Him whom I love, then the 2 Corinthians passage becomes hateful instead of helpful. The verses I will share in the last chapter are special ones that keep me in close relationship with Him and that make me want to be called to His standards.

To God be all glory and honor and blessing and power for all He has done—and for all He continues to do.

Chapter One

The Context and the Text

A re you ready for what could be the biggest "Well, duh!" of Bible teaching? Get this: The book of Second Corinthians was written after the book of First Corinthians. Here's something not quite so dumb: The part of Second Corinthians we are studying refers back to the content of First Corinthians. Not all of it does; part of it deals with entirely new subjects to instruct and encourage the church at Corinth.

Much of First Corinthians dealt with problems in the church in the city of Corinth. This included divisions, immorality, lawsuits between believers, marriage and divorce, eating food sacrificed to idols, conduct in worship, the Lord's Supper, the use of spiritual gifts, and misunderstandings about the resurrection of Christians.

Second Corinthians addressed some additional issues such as the apostolic authority of Paul, the giving of funds, and being yoked to unbelievers.

However, a major message is how delighted Paul was about the response of the church to the first letter. He had been somewhat fearful that it would cause great grief and possible damage. By God's grace the Corinthians had responded well and were now eager to receive Paul, whom they had previously wished to avoid. Our longer text, and of course the shorter text within the longer, was written as part of this almost ecstatic praise. Verses eight and nine are preparatory sentences. Verse ten and most of verse eleven are the text that we will examine in subsequent chapters.

I encourage you to refer back to this chapter regularly. As we examine the results of godly sorrow, compare the various words and phrases chosen by the translators or paraphrasers of the different versions.

2 Corinthians 7:8–11 (KJV): For though I made you sorry with a letter, I do not repent, though I did repent for I perceive that the same epistle hath made you sorry, though it were but for a season. Now I rejoice, not that ye were made sorry, but that ye sorrowed to repentance: for ye were made sorry after a godly manner, that ye might receive damage by us in nothing. *For godly sorrow worketh repentance to salvation not to be repented of: but the sorrow of the world worketh death. For behold this self-same*

thing, that ye sorrowed after a godly sort, what care-
fulness it wrought in you, yea, what clearing of your-
selves, yea, what indignation, yea, what fear, yea, what
vehement desire, yea, what zeal, yea, what revenge! In
all these things you have approved yourselves to be
clear in this matter. (Italics mine)

2 Corinthians 7:8–11 (NIV): Even if I caused you
sorrow by my letter, I do not regret it. Though I did
regret it—I see that my letter hurt you, but only for
a little while—yet now I am happy, not because you
were made sorry, but because your sorrow led you
to repentance. For you became sorrowful as God
intended and so were not harmed in any way by us.
Godly sorrow brings repentance that leads to salvation
and leaves no regret, but worldly sorrow brings death.
See what this godly sorrow has produced in you: what
earnestness, what eagerness to clear yourselves, what
indignation, what alarm, what longing, what concern,
what readiness to see justice done. At every point you
have proved yourself to be innocent in this matter.
(Italics mine)

2 Corinthians 7:10–11 (NKJV): For godly sorrow
produces repentance to salvation, not to be regret-
ted; but the sorrow of the world produces death.
For observe this very thing, that you sorrowed in a
godly manner: What diligence it produced in you,
what clearing of yourselves, what indignation, what

fear, what vehement desire, what zeal, what vindication!

2 Corinthians 7:10–11 (ASV): For godly sorrow worketh repentance unto salvation, a repentance which bringeth no regret: but the sorrow of the world worketh death. For behold, this selfsame thing, that ye were made sorry after a godly sort, what earnest care it wrought in you, yea what clearing of yourselves, yea what indignation, yea what fear, yea what longing, yea what zeal, yea what avenging!

2 Corinthians 7:10–11 (NASB): For the sorrow that is according to the will of God produces a repentance without regret, leading to salvation; but the sorrow of the world produces death. For behold what earnestness this very thing, this godly sorrow, has produced in you: what vindication of yourselves, what indignation, what fear, what longing, what zeal, what avenging of wrong!

2 Corinthians 7:10–11 (TEV): For the sadness that is used by God brings a change of heart that leads to salvation—and there is no regret in that! But sadness that is merely human causes death. See what God did with this sadness of yours: how earnest it has made you, how eager to prove your innocence! Such indignation, such alarm, such feelings, such devotion, such readiness to punish wrongdoing!

2 Corinthians 7:10–11 (RSV): For godly sorrow produces a repentance that leads to salvation and brings no regret, but worldly grief produces death. For see what earnestness this godly grief has produced in you, what eagerness to clear yourselves, what indignation, what alarm, what longing, what zeal, what punishment!

2 Corinthians 7:10–11 (Phillips): The sorrow which God uses means a change of heart and leads to salvation—it is the world's sorrow that is such a deadly thing. You can look back now and see how the hand of God was in that sorrow. Look how seriously it made you think, how eager it made you to prove your innocence, how indignant it made you, and in some cases how afraid! Look how it made you long for my presence, how it stirred up your keenness for the faith, how ready it made you to punish the offender!

2 Corinthians 7:10–11 (Williams): For the sorrow that comes in accordance with the will of God results in repentance that leads to salvation and leaves no regrets; but the sorrow the world produces results in death. For see what this very sorrow, suffered in accordance with the will of God, has done for you! How earnest it has made you, how concerned to clear yourselves, how indignant, how alarmed, how much it made you long to see me,

how loyal to me, how determined to punish the offender!

2 Corinthians 7:10–11 (Beck): Being sad in God's way makes you feel sorry for sin so as to save you— you can't regret that. But the sorrow of the world brings death. See how eager God's sorrow has made you, how ready to clear yourselves, how disgusted with wrong, how alarmed you were, what longing and zeal you felt, and how ready you were to punish!

2 Corinthians 7:10–11 (NEB): For the wound which is borne in God's way brings a change of heart too salutary to regret; but the hurt which is borne in the world's way brings death. You bore your hurt in God's way and see what its results have been! It made you take the matter seriously and vindicate yourselves. How angered you were, how apprehensive! How your longing for me awoke, yes, and your devotion and your eagerness to see justice done!

2 Corinthians 7:10–11 (The Amplified Bible): For godly grief *and* the pain God is permitted to direct, produce a repentance that leads *and* contributes to salvation *and* deliverance from evil, and it never brings regret; but worldly grief [the hopeless sorrow that is characteristic of the pagan world] is deadly— breeding *and* ending in death. For [you can look back now and] observe what this same godly *sorrow*

has done for you *and* has produced in you: what eagerness and earnest care *to* explain *and* clear yourselves [of all complicity in the condoning of incest], what indignation [at the sin], what alarm, what yearning, what zeal [to do justice to all concerned], what readiness to mete out punishment [to the offender]!

2 Corinthians 7:10–11 (CEV): When God makes you feel sorry enough to turn to him and be saved, you don't have anything to feel bad about. But when this world makes you feel sorry, it can cause your death. Just look what God has done by making you feel sorry! You sincerely want to prove that you are innocent. You are angry. You are shocked. You are eager to see that justice is done.

2 Corinthians 7:10–11 (NLT): For God can use sorrow in our lives to help us turn away from sin and seek salvation. We will never regret that kind of sorrow. But sorrow without repentance is the kind that results in death. Just see what this godly sorrow produced in you! Such earnestness, such concern to clear yourselves, such indignation, such alarm, such longing to see me, such zeal, and such a readiness to punish the wrongdoer.

2 Corinthians 7:10–11 (The Living Bible): For God sometimes uses sorrow in our lives to help us turn away from sin and seek eternal life. We should never

regret His sending it. But the sorrow of the man who is not a Christian is not the sorrow of true repentance and does not prevent eternal death. Just see how much good this grief from the Lord did for you! You no longer shrugged your shoulders, but became earnest and sincere, and very anxious to get rid of the sin that I wrote you about. You became frightened about what had happened and longed for me to come and help. You went right to work on the problem and cleared it up [punishing the man who sinned].

2 Corinthians 7:10–11 (The Message): Distress that drives us to God does that. It turns us around. It gets us back in the way of salvation. We never regret that kind of pain. But those who let distress drive them away from God are full of regret, end up on a deathbed of regrets. And now, isn't it wonderful all the ways in which this distress has goaded you closer to God? You're more alive, more concerned, more sensitive, more reverent, more human, more passionate, more responsible.

Chapter Two

Godly Sorrow
Brings Repentance

Have you ever asked someone if he is a Christian? There are lots of ways to do so. One is the direct phrase I just used. It would bring an affirmative response from most Americans. After all, even though we have freedom of religion and are home to many Jews, Muslims, Hindus, Buddhists, Satanists, and other obvious non-Christians, most Americans are Protestant, Catholic or Orthodox; and though we would question their claims, the Mormons, Jehovah's Witnesses, and many New Agers would also classify themselves as Christians.

Sometimes we try to ask the same question in a more defining way. "Have you been born again?" "Do you know Jesus as your personal Savior?" "If you died tonight, do you know for sure you would go to heaven?"

When we believe someone truly is a child of God, a born-again Christian, we may ask how he came to this experience. Most of those to whom I have talked allude quickly to one of two factors as they give their testimony: either they realized that they had no relationship with God, and felt horribly empty; or they recognized their sinfulness, and felt condemned. It was either their emptiness or their sense of sinfulness that caused them to aggressively seek God.

I believe that many who came from the emptiness position soon (or eventually) realized that they actually were coming from a position of sinfulness. I was one of these. When I first heard the gospel as a university student, I was attending a school that, according to one international magazine, had the highest per capita alcohol consumption of any university in the world. There were a lot of other problems that accompanied that much alcohol. I was one of the few "good" kids. I drank less than most. I didn't smoke, didn't do drugs, and was not sexually active. I was even a serious student and one of the less than ten percent who attended church. I did not see myself as sinful, but as empty. When alone in my room I prayed and asked Jesus into my life, I had a glimmer that emptiness was not my only problem—but only a glimmer. I asked for forgiveness of sins, but in a superficial way. It was just the thing to do.

Jesus answered my prayer for relationship and came into my life. Some effects were almost immediate. One was an almost insatiable desire to study the Bible. I spent over an hour each day reading Scripture. As a result, I very quickly came to realize that what I had perceived as emptiness was really a result of my sin that had separated me from God. I realized I had not just been wandering, but I was truly lost—condemned, guilty, bound for hell. I marveled at the magnificence of God's grace and of Jesus' sacrifice for me. As I began to mature in my spiritual walk, I recognized how destructive sin had been, and how destructive it *could* be. I sought and found the resources to battle and overcome temptation through the abiding presence of the Holy Spirit. I wish the victory was just as quick and complete as I just made it sound—for it is actually an ongoing process, and I have come before God to repent and confess specific sins many times.

I very soon came to experience what I believe Paul meant by "godly sorrow." I hated and grieved over my sinfulness and the sins I committed as a result. I was torn between the desire to keep confessing, and repenting, and asking for forgiveness for what was past, and the desire to praise Him because He had in fact forgiven all those trespasses and shortcomings. Fortunately, God showed me through His Word that the blood of Jesus had totally cleansed me. The Holy Spirit had indeed made me a new creation in Christ (2 Corinthians 5:17). I joyously praised Him for what He had done and what He promised He would continue to do.

I soon began to see the difference between confession and repentance. Confession was agreeing with God about the sinfulness of sin. I have talked with people who tell me how smoking or drinking or taking drugs is killing them. They are confessing what is true, but the confession is meaningless because there is no change. I have also talked to some on a spiritual level who confess that they are lost, but they have no desire to change. They too are making a true confession of their spiritual state. However, confession is completely inadequate without repentance. Repentance is a renunciation of sins and a deliberate choice to stop. It leads to change!

Godly sorrow *includes* confession. It is agreeing with God about ourselves and our condition, and being positively miserable about what He says and what He shows us. But godly sorrow also includes *conviction.* This is a good old-fashioned evangelical word describing what the Holy Spirit does to show us our need for Christ. It is essentially the same in the legal and spiritual senses: to be "convicted" means we are found to be guilty. When the Holy Spirit convicts us, we are beyond confessing what we have done. Now we bear the guilt. The trial is over. The next step would be the sentencing, except for the fact that Jesus has intervened for us and has taken our sentence upon Himself. This leads to *repentance,* in which we declare that we need to change and that we *will* change. (It reminds me of Ebenezer Scrooge, who was transformed after meeting the three spirits of Christmas Past, Christmas Present, and Christmas Future.)

Many who are stumbling have cried that they repent and repent and repent, and are unable to change! In some cases it is because they have not received Jesus as their Savior and therefore don't have the spiritual resources for change. In other cases these are truly born-again believers, but they still cannot find the victory over the particular sin or sins that overcome them so consistently. In my ministering to such people, the Lord has sometimes clearly shown them why they are being defeated and they have then chosen (or rejected) the steps to victory. For others, the answer has not come so easily—so I seek to encourage them to keep fighting and not to give up until the Lord does give the answer, which in His grace and time He does. In my own life-experience, victory in some areas has been virtually instantaneous because the desire that empowered the sin was gone. In other areas the victory was not as quick, and in still others the struggle lasted for years—and I'm certainly not perfect yet. But on the whole, the transformation in my life is easily as great as that of Ebenezer Scrooge, and it is continuing. One of my favorite verses is Romans 8:29: "Those whom God foreknew He predestined to be conformed to the image of Christ." This conforming will not be complete until we die and are finally fully transformed into His likeness as we see Him face to face. That will be the *final* perfecting. In the meantime, if we believe and appropriate Romans 8:29, we can become so Christlike that those around us will truly see Christ in us. Another wonderful verse is Hebrews 10:14, which expresses simultaneously the ideas of the completed and continuing aspects of God's working in our lives: "By one sacrifice He has made perfect forever those who are being made holy."

Godly sorrow leads to repentance; seeing as God sees leads to *change*. Paul goes on to say that this repentance is not to be repented of—in other words, it is good. And godly sorrow causes us to *hate* sin, not merely dislike it. We live with many things we dislike because we are not willing to make the effort necessary to get rid of them. However, we are much more likely to expend great energy and effort to get rid of something we hate.

I came to Christ in 1969, back when preaching in many evangelical churches focused strongly on the sinfulness of sin and its horrible social and eternal consequences. "Altar calls" were common. People were exhorted to go to the altar and repent and find salvation. Tears of sorrow were shed, followed by shouts or exclamations of joy as the sinner found forgiveness. The godly sorrow was a burden much like that experienced by Christian in *Pilgrim's Progress*—the weight and awareness of which nearly wore him down, until it finally rolled away at the cross of Christ and disappeared, never to be seen again.

Not everyone urged to come responds with such zeal. Many people will ask, "If I become a Christian, can I still. . . ." There are many things they want to continue which they feel are probably wrong, but they want to negotiate. They want forgiveness of sins, but they also want to maintain control of their lives. They acknowledge that they themselves have caused their problems, but they feel that if they were forgiven they could do a better job the second, or third, or fiftieth time when it comes to running their own lives. There is no *real* repentance, just a desire for safety. In Acts 16, Luke gives us a great example of true conversion. Paul and Silas, he tells us, were unjustly imprisoned in Philippi. At midnight they were singing praises and praying—which they had probably been doing for quite a while—after having been severely flogged and their feet put into the stocks. Then an earthquake occurs and the prisoners' chains

are unfastened, and the jailer—having barely been
stopped by Paul from killing himself—rushes to the
apostles not with any desire to negotiate, but with
one loud cry, "What must I do to be *saved*!" (Acts
16:30). It was a cry of desperation!

Sometimes we don't really understand Paul's
reply. In the NKJV he declares, "Believe on the Lord
Jesus Christ, and you will be saved" (Acts 16:31).
"Believe"—that sure sounds easy. It wasn't. Let me
paraphrase what Paul was saying and show you what
the jailer understood him to say: "If you want to be
saved, you have to believe and acknowledge that
Jesus, the Messiah, is *Lord of all.* You can no longer,
as a Roman jailer, say 'Caesar is Lord,' but you must
acknowledge *Jesus.* If you do that, you may find
yourself in this same prison, but you will have eternal life!" What was the jailer's response? He believed
and was baptized, openly identifying himself with
Jesus. He was not trying to walk in two worlds, in
which he could be confident of both physical and
spiritual safety. He chose Jesus and *only* Jesus. Why?
Because in essence he had experienced godly sorrow, and so he responded appropriately. Godly sorrow led to repentance, which led to the two parts of
salvation—forgiveness of sins and a new life in Jesus.

There may be less preaching now on sin, guilt,
and judgment than in my youthful days. Conver-
sions now often seem more moral than spiritual.

Pollsters tell us that many students, and their pro-
fessors—even in many Christian liberal arts col-
leges—do not believe in a literal hell or in the possibility of being eternally condemned and separated
from God. Therefore there is no need to make Jesus
Lord of their lives, since there is little or nothing to
fear by not doing so. Since these students are generally from church backgrounds, they may well be
reflecting what they are taught, or what they are *not*
taught, if hell and judgment are ignored. Around
the year 1990, the Dean of Students at a very conservative Christian liberal arts college (that is affili-
ated with a noted conservative denomination) told
me that until the mid-1980's the arrival of the freshman class meant an influx of dynamic, excited young
people eager to grow spiritually and learn academi-
cally. Their arrival was always a spiritual boost for
the other classes. Then around the mid-1980's there
was a change. Students were coming from the same
churches, but much of the chapel activity during
the first semester was spent working to get many of
the freshman class converted. Something had
changed!

Less teaching on sin has led to less godly sorrow
and less repentance than in previous generations. It
may even lead to less salvation, because if we talk of
receiving Jesus without meeting His conditions, we
may be giving false assurance. For those who truly

do come to Christ, less teaching on true repentance may cause less or slower spiritual growth, especially if they are coming from a perceived point of emptiness—as I initially did—rather than from a point of sinfulness. Would we tell such people that their "faith" is insufficient and they are unsaved? I don't think so. I believe that in these cases we need to help these infant Christians—who have truly believed the message they have heard—to study the Word of God. Don't just tell them to go and read it on their own. Study *with them.* God will use His Word, enlightened by His Spirit, to convict and convince and conform them. "Faith comes from hearing the message, and the message is heard through the word of Christ" (Romans 10:17). This truth applies not only to *saving* faith that comes through hearing (or reading) the Word of God, it also applies to a *growing* faith, such as found in new or immature Christians—and to growth, likewise, in the most *mature* believers. The serious study of Scripture will lead to the godly sorrow that leads to lasting repentance and a transformed, *maturing* life.

Another way to look at this is by comparing it with ministry to children. Many WEC missionaries whom I have interviewed "accepted Jesus" as young children—often as young as four or five years old. Later they acknowledged that their understanding was limited, and their commitment, while sincere, was in no way based on an "adult" understanding. Yet as they matured in age and learned more of the Bible and Jesus, they matured spiritually. In almost every case (I say "almost" though I don't know of any exceptions) they came to a point where they really understood the power of sin, and the greater power of Jesus. They then made the type of commitment that enabled them to respond to God's later leading to become missionaries. This understanding could well be described as a "godly sorrow" experience that included repentance for what had been an inconsistent life, of which they were not proud. They repented of trying to please God and others equally, or even of having given God second place.

Godly sorrow leads to repentance which leads to salvation and subsequent spiritual growth. In the next seven chapters we will look at seven results of a genuine salvation. As I have studied these effects, I feel that they are listed in an order that expresses increased intensity or emotion, and perhaps even action, as we go from one to the next.

Chapter Three

What Carefulness;
What Earnestness!

Godly sorrow led the Corinthians to repentance which in turn led to this first result. The KJV calls it "carefulness." The NIV calls it "earnestness." I encourage you to flip back to Chapter One to see how the other versions handle this first characteristic. You will find one that seems to combine both ideas by saying "earnest care." Another uses "diligence." Phillips says, ". . . how seriously it made you think." This is the first step in a deeper spiritual walk.

Why are we careful or earnest or diligent or serious? Perhaps, like the Philippian jailer, we realize that the being we basically thought of as a god or as "god" is really "God" and in fact more like "GOD." He is greater, bigger, more majestic, more worthy, more "GOD-LIKE" than I can comprehend, and I realize how *nothing I* am in comparison. I realize that Ananias and Sapphira lied to Him and died (Acts 5). I realize God is a consuming fire (Hebrews 12:29) and I am not naturally fireproof. *He* is the Judge and *He* has set the standards for judgment. I realize my own sin corrupted me so much that my only escape was through the death of Jesus, God's Son. An angel was not sufficient, not even Gabriel or Michael. Only One who was *perfect* could become sin for me so I could be forgiven. God has become so wonderful and so horrible that He is scary either way. I have repented of carelessness and lukewarmness. I need to take God as seriously as He takes Himself.

What does it mean to be careful in a way I was not before? Before I experienced the godly sorrow that led to such a change, I might see something about which God said "Do not touch," and give a little touch anyway. I felt it was okay to see a little evil, hear a little evil, or speak a little evil. I wasn't doing anything terrible—I was more spiritual than many around me. Holiness was for someday; accommodation was for today. After all, if I was too spiritual, or fanatical, or freaky weird, no one would listen to me if I talked about Jesus.

What really happened was that I came to realize that while sin may not have the same consequences for a Christian as for a non-Christian, it would still leave me stunted and groping in obscurity rather than joyously and confidently walking in light. I would be struggling through a muddy valley rather than leaping on high places. I could not experience the fullness of the Holy Spirit if I was filling myself with garbage. God has high standards for those who call themselves His. He also gave us all we need in order to attain these standards. Just as it took the death of the only One capable of bearing our sin and guilt in order for us to be forgiven, so God has given us the only One capable of living a holy life to actually dwell within us. Just as God died for us in the Person of His Son, so He lives in us in the Person of the Holy Spirit. We have everything we need for life and godliness (2 Peter 1:3). "Everything" still means what it always did—everything. Nothing is missing. We participate in (are partakers of) the divine nature (2 Peter 1:4). Therefore we add to our faith goodness, knowledge, self-control, perseverance, godliness, brotherly kindness, and love (2 Peter 1:5–7).

Let's look at it another way. I had known God, or rather had known about God, but it was in a religious, especially-on-Sunday, superficial way. He was like the neighbor I saw only occasionally. I was satisfied because I had what I wanted and He seemed satisfied. I figured I could find Him if I needed Him, and I was pleased He was near, but not too near. After all, I needed my spiritual "personal space" just like I need it in the world.

Now I have come to know Him as I never dreamed possible. Now I love Him with all my heart and soul and mind and strength, and I would rather die than have this relationship diminish. I want Him to set the standards and I want high ones so I can show how eager I am to serve Him. I don't want Him to be disappointed in me. Does this sound like the immaturity of a child trying to please a parent? Not so! I am not trying to please a parent in order to win approval or love, but I want to please my Father whose approval and love I already have and by whose approval and love I am overwhelmed! It is *maturity* rather than immaturity. Remember Scrooge? He felt giddy and free. He wanted to leap and celebrate. So he did! But remember, Scrooge still ran his business and probably continued to make lots of money . . . even though he now treated people as God meant them to be treated. In the same way, we have the joy of the Lord whom we know intimately and love intensely even while we carry on with our jobs and relationships.

I am careful and earnest because not only do I not want to have my relationship with God diminish (or my vision of Him to become dim), but I also cannot stand the thought of others seeing GOD as anything less than He is because of my life. His honor and reputation and wonderful name are at stake! It is bad enough that God is dishonored by the majority of the men and women He created and loves and sent His Son to redeem. It would be absolutely unbearable that He should be dishonored through my life and actions. I realize God is big enough to take care of Himself, and that eventually His name will be honored by all; but there is no way it is honorable for *me* to dishonor Him. I care how my life affects the reputation of my family; I care a lot more how my life affects the reputation of my heavenly Father!

What about fear? That seems to be a good motivator. I have already used the example of Ananias and Sapphira. I used the scriptural description of God as a consuming fire. Sudden death and burning, however, do not seem compatible with *love*.

Fear does motivate. Chapter Six will deal specifically with this topic. But fear is a motivator that can create resentment and even hatred. The one who is subject to fear generally looks for a way to escape, not to draw closer. Fear serves well as a short-term motivator. For example, it might encourage me not to lie. It may keep me from sinning or disobeying. But it is *love* that makes serving God a joy, and makes obedience a pleasure. Like C.T. Studd in the Introduction, we are looking for commands from God because we want to *obey* Him.

Several of those converted while Linda and I were

in Guinea-Bissau illustrate the motivation of love. Most of those who sought to be converted had not been convinced by someone's preaching but rather by "proofs"—the seekers were usually family members, friends, or co-workers of those who had *already* come to Jesus! Those previously converted had occasionally endured varying levels of persecution and had stood firm. That caught the attention of those who knew them. In some cases, individuals had experienced healings, provisions, or other blessings that were obviously from God. They had shared their testimonies of God's goodness and as a result others wanted to become "believers."

As I would talk with those wanting to join us I asked a lot of questions. It became obvious that in almost every case, they did not really understand the gospel. They wanted Jesus because of what they could *not* get from their present religion, whether Islam or Animism. This included forgiveness of sins as well as some obvious temporal blessings, but neither religion provided a biblical concept of sin. Therefore I would inform them that they had to study with me for an extended period of time, often up to a couple of hours a day for two weeks, so I could be sure they knew what they were seeking and what it might cost them.

A good bit of time would be spent discussing sin, the source of sin, and the power of sin. It was not at all hard to convince them they had a sinful nature; it was obvious in many aspects of their lives and culture. Furthermore, as they became more and more aware of their guilt, they became positively discouraged. And when we talked about the wages of sin, they would not argue that they deserved a break or that it wasn't their fault—they went from discouraged to hopeless. Then we began with the *good* news.

We talked of God in all His GODLINESS. *You* define that. Imagine the biggest, best, most glorious, most loving, almighty, eternal GOD you can, then talk about His qualities and attributes. That's what I mean by GODLY in capital letters. The more time you spend thinking, the more wonderful He becomes! Then we talked of Jesus and His divinity, His sacrificial death, His resurrection, His present intercession, and His guaranteed return. Yes, this was what they wanted, *but* I had convinced them so well of their sinfulness that they knew they could not live the life this righteous God would require . . . so He would probably have to abandon or destroy them! At the very least, they would constantly live in fear of His impending wrath.

Then we began to talk of the Holy Spirit. We told how just as God and Jesus are divine, so is He. We talked about how God planned for our salvation, how Jesus was the instrument of our salvation,

and how the Holy Spirit is the *assurance* of our salvation because He *lives* in us. After a while it was
obvious they were beginning to understand. They
already had the concept of evil spirits indwelling
people; they fully accepted demon possession as a
fact. Spirit possession was part of their former belief
system. Some acquaintances they knew to be possessed in such a way that they had supernatural pow-
ers, and others were almost dehumanized. Many
had friends they felt to be occasionally possessed
and nearly normal the rest of the time. We talked
about the fact that Satan could not dwell in anyone
unless he had a legal right, since God had created
everyone. That legal right was *sin*. All have sinned;
therefore Satan has the legal right to dwell in everyone . . . and he does have spiritual *control* of everyone whether it shows dramatically in terms of ap-
parent possession or merely in the inability to consistently do what is right.

But Jesus *redeemed us*. He took our sin and our
guilt. Satan had to leave! But wouldn't that leave us
empty? What about the parable in Matthew 12 in
which an evil spirit left a man (probably because it
was forced to), wandered about, found no place to
settle, and so returned to its previous host and took
seven worse spirits with it? The man was worse off
than he was before. Jesus does *not* leave us empty,
however; He sends His own Spirit to fill us. He fully

fills us. Therefore Satan does not have room to get in. He can stand outside and yell and lie and roar and threaten, but he cannot get in!

At this point they really understood the gospel and wanted the forgiveness of Jesus and the fullness of the Holy Spirit. A love for the Father and the Son came very easily. *This* was the motivation that held them to the gospel. They knew they would become more than overcomers through Him who lives in them. Of course, they knew that although they would be free from Satan's control, they would be subject to God. That idea was a delight! A God who cared enough for them to become man and *die* for them could only be One who would *continue* to love them. There was no fear in making a total commitment to One who is a loving Father. They understood that the covenant the Father was making with them was one that gives freedom (James 2:12), not one that would make them miserable.

In the Old Testament the Jews were constantly reminded to "be careful" to obey all the requirements of the Law. This demonstrated their earnestness. When they failed, they were required to bring an appropriate sacrifice to acknowledge their sin and show repentance. It was when they quit being "careful" to serve God that they began to serve idols. This led to their destruction.

Love for my Father, my Savior, and my present

Comforter causes *me* to be careful. It is not a fearful, tiptoe-on-eggshells-and-keep-a-low-profile carefulness. It is a *confident* carefulness. It is a carefulness that leads naturally to the next characteristic.

Chapter Four

What Clearing of Yourselves; What Eagerness to Clear Yourselves!

T he first result of the repentance that was the fruit of godly sorrow was "carefulness" or "earnestness." The next step is what we will consider in this chapter, for which both the KJV and NIV give the idea of "clearing yourselves." Simply put, this means trying to make right what you have done wrong. This often includes apology and restitution. Each of these requires a humbling of our hearts and a deliberate action.

When Linda and I were first married we lived in Rarden, Ohio. We rented a very small house behind the home of "Doc" and Hazel Gardner. This house had originally been a summer kitchen, to which a tiny bathroom and a bedroom had been added. (For those of you too young to know what a summer kitchen was, I'll explain. In the days before air conditioning, cooking in the summer made the house extremely hot. Many families constructed a separate but nearby building in which most of the cooking was done during those months. The cooked food was then brought into the main house for eating. In cooler times of the year the heat from the primary kitchen was welcomed in the main house, so the extra kitchen was simply closed until the summer returned.)

When I first met Doc it was easy to tell he was unconverted. However, he was a very good landlord and I tried to be a very good tenant. It seemed Doc just had to get converted. I was the Methodist minister living on the same property. Doc's brother and sister lived in the two houses on each side of Doc and Hazel. His brother was a Baptist and his sister a Nazarene. Both were strong believers. Finally, Doc got converted. There was no doubt of his conversion. He was transformed!

Although Doc and Hazel went to the Nazarene church after his conversion, he and I spent a lot of time talking and praying together because the Nazarene minister had a full-time nonministerial job and lived a fair distance away. I was privileged to watch him mature rapidly in his faith.

Within a week of his conversion Doc was driving all over the countryside. He asked God to show him people to whom he had lied, from whom he had stolen, whom he had offended, or anything else along that line. There were a lot! So he went to each of these personally to ask forgiveness for what he had done and to make things right. He knew God had forgiven him, but he wanted to be "clear" with everyone. Some people hated and feared Doc so much that they didn't want to see him when he arrived. It took him a while to convince them even to talk to him! Later, after confession, apology, and restitution if appropriate, Doc was able to share his faith with people who were absolutely convinced of his new life in Jesus.

A somewhat sad footnote is that Doc only lived about two years after his conversion. He was a good guitarist and a fair singer. He often used these talents in his Nazarene church, and in any other church in which revival services were being held. One night after singing a song, Doc said that nothing could make him happier than to die on the spot and go to be with Jesus. Almost as soon as the words were out of his mouth, that was exactly what happened!

I too went through some "clearing of myself" after my conversion. Although I was not as outwardly wicked as Doc had been, I had certain things I had to clear. Since I was living in Germany and most of these involved people back in America, I had to do most of it by mail.

I had been in Cub Scouts, Boy Scouts, and then Explorers. My final contact had been working as a counselor at a camp the last summer I was in America. I taught rifle and archery to the campers. One afternoon a small group of counselors talked about how to steal goods from the camp store. We obviously had to do it at night; the trick was how to get into a locked building. I found a way and we stole about a hundred dollars worth of items. Although the theft was discovered when an inventory was made, we were never caught. This was the fall of 1966. I was converted in January of 1968 and almost immediately I knew I had to contact the Boy Scouts. I was honestly concerned that I might be arrested, but I wanted a clear heart. So I wrote to the office in Colorado where the camp had been, confessed my part, and sent money to pay for what I had stolen. Of course I explained why I was doing this. Instead of an arrest warrant, I received a letter in which the writer expressed happiness about my conversion and act of restitution. The money would be used to help pay for campers who could not afford the fees.

I attended my first two years of high school in Fayetteville, North Carolina. Although I was a fairly good student I had a problem with Biology in grade ten. I think I simply got too involved with non-scholastic activities to study as I should. On one test I decided to cheat. I got caught and taken to the office of the vice-principal, Percy Warren. I was able to convince him that I was not cheating but that when I lifted the top of my desk ever so slightly, I was looking for something—it was merely "coincidence" that the notes I was review-ing immediately before the test were there! I was actually astounded that I could look him in the eyes and lie, but I did. I wrote to Mr. Warren from Germany to confess that I had cheated and had lied to him. I asked his forgiveness.

Those were not the only things I had to do to "clear" myself, but they suffice as examples. I have heard a number of people say that when they re-ceived Jesus as Savior, God forgave their sins and so they had no intention of asking forgiveness from people. For Doc Gardner, for me, and apparently for the believers in the church at Corinth, God led differently. It could be easily argued that the key factor is *God's leading.* I agree. But I would also add that when God gives a clear principle, *that* is often His leading; and we should respond as He brings specific circumstances to mind. Fear and pride were the two main obstacles I had to overcome. Once I did as He led, the joy and peace and sense of well-being made the obstacles seem like nothing.

Perhaps this principle of "clearing" can be ex-pressed in another way. Nothing is hidden from

God—and at the time when we stand before Him, everything will be presented. What does this have to do with us now? Many Christians live in fear of things they have done becoming known. Yet this kind of fear is contrary to the freedom we are to find in Christ. One response is to say that this is certainly "under the blood" of Jesus, and therefore since God has forgiven it, I will forget it. If God gives an individual the ability, freedom and peace to do this, I say amen. For those who are not finding an ability to forget, then it may be that God is getting their attention because He wants them to confess and to make restitution if possible. God does not lead every person the same way. He leads each one in the way that is best for him and best for His overall plan.

There are two kinds of guilt. The first is what we often call "false guilt." This is generally first brought on by teachers who outline a litany of sins and then demand a uniform response from all who are hearing them, or reading what they have written. The hearers and readers are directed to aggressively ask God to show them every sin they have committed, of which there are surely many. Then these are to be confessed, either to God or another, and there may or may not be accompanying restitution demanded. Furthermore, the listeners or readers are often told how weak and wicked they still are, due to their "flesh" or "carnal natures," so they have to keep coming to God to seek forgiveness for the many sins they will even yet commit. The result: *someone else* becomes our conscience, instead of our allowing the Holy Spirit to guide us. We never become fully free. We struggle with a burden of feeling unforgiven, or forgiven but certain of ongoing sinfulness. If this pattern becomes established, Satan is glad to get involved and constantly whisper to us about our perceived sinfulness. Our Christian walk becomes characterized by *misery* rather than joy, *bondage* rather than freedom.

At this point, I could easily switch horses in the middle on the proverbial stream and write chapter after chapter elaborating on our new birth, the new person we have become, the new nature of which we are partakers, and the whole new way of living and understanding who we are in Christ; but I won't. The purpose of this chapter is to deal with the concept of experiencing what Paul has called the "clearing of ourselves"—as a positive result of the godly sorrow the Holy Spirit brings to us.

The Holy Spirit does not ordinarily if ever convict Christians of a general sinfulness in terms of forgiveness and restitution. He convicts of *specific* sins so that these may be confessed and forgiven and forgotten. If there is an appropriate action to be taken, He shows this. This is what I'll call "true guilt" in contrast to the false guilt of two paragraphs ago. False guilt leads to bondage and puts us on a treadmill of conviction and confession that never ends, and makes us miserable in our attempt to please God. He becomes the Parent who is never satisfied. True guilt also makes us miserable, but when we respond to God we find forgiveness, joy, peace and rest in the embrace of our Father, who loves us enough to make us face the truth. There is a wonderful cleansing when we come to God through Jesus for the forgiveness of sins in the crisis of the new birth. There is a similar and very real sense of cleansing as we obey the Spirit and clear past sins and offenses we have committed against others!

In summary, there are three possible reactions to the sins of our past. The *first* is a mental declaration that since God has forgiven me, there is nothing to confess to others—and certainly no need for restitution. The *second* is a morbid sense that I am never fully forgiven, because I continue in the weakness (some would say sinfulness) of my pre-Christian past. I confess, make restitution, and vainly struggle to enjoy the love of Jesus. The *third* is a sensitivity to the Holy Spirit and an ability to distinguish His voice from that of Satan. When He convicts, I respond; and this response leads to freedom. If there is restitution involved, it not only strengthens my relationship with my Father but it is often used redemptively in the lives of others.

The first characteristic of a new life in Christ is a carefulness to keep from sinning. The second characteristic is an eagerness to have a clear relationship with God and with all people. This comes not from covering up the past, but by apology and restitution. This leads to the third characteristic, a healthy and proper attitude toward both sin and temptation. That is what we shall look at next.

Chapter Five

What Indignation!

One reason for my quoting a variety of different versions in Chapter One is to give a variety of synonyms and ways of expressing each of the seven results of the repentance that flows from godly sorrow. The third response, "indignation," seems to be special. Almost every true translation (versus paraphrase) uses either "indignation" or "indignant." The NEB and CEV use a different word, "angered" or "angry," while Beck renders it "disgusted with wrong."

How do we define, describe, or illustrate indignation? The American College Dictionary defines indignation as "displeasure at something deemed unworthy, unjust, or base; righteous anger."

I was interested in the last part of the definition. I have heard of "righteous indignation" all my life. If we put that phrase with this definition we would have righteous righteous anger, or doubly righteous anger, or truly righteous anger. Does such anger exist? Jesus seemed to exemplify it when He chased the money changers and merchants from the temple grounds. When Jesus healed the man with the withered hand (Mark 3:1–6) He was angered at the stubborn hearts of those who were opposed to the concept of doing good on the Sabbath. Since Jesus did not sin, His anger was righteous, directed at something He deemed unworthy, unjust, and perhaps even base. Another word for His anger in this situation would be "indignation."

According to our primary text, indignation is one of the results, the third listed, in someone who has responded appropriately to godly sorrow brought by the Holy Spirit. This person is now careful in his walk with God and before men. He is working to clear himself with others for his actions and attitudes from the past. Now he is squarely facing daily life. How does he feel and act when confronted by temptations and by the fruit of sin in our society and world? An appropriate response is indignation—righteous anger at something unworthy, unjust, or base.

What is temptation? It is a suggestion by Satan to do something to disobey or dishonor God. That is always unworthy. It is certainly unjust. If we could see it as God sees it, I believe we would know it is always base, no matter how beautiful or pleasing Satan might make it appear.

So how do we respond with indignation? When

Jesus was indignant because the Jews around Him did not want Him to heal the man with the withered hand, He healed him! He did something about the situation. When Paul was indignant (my interpretation) about the way Peter was acting around Gentile believers (Galatians 2:11–14), he confronted him! He initiated change in the situation.

As a parent and husband there are things that make me indignant. Advertising about certain television shows feature suggestions that the show will have sexual humor and vulgarity. My reaction is that I don't watch the show even once. As a teenager I once heard another teen make a suggestive comment about my younger sister. I became indignant, and he felt it appropriate to apologize. I am indignant about the things that affect my wife and children. By God's grace I am becoming indignant about things that affect society and the world as a whole. In fact, one of the specific things that led me to be a missionary was grief (or indignation) over the fact that most people in Guinea-Bissau were on the way to hell and had never had a chance to hear the gospel. This situation had to be changed! Linda and I went to change it.

Earnestness or carefulness was the first lasting response to godly sorrow. (Actually the very first response was, of course, the repentance that brought me to Jesus.) Carefulness thus became a lifestyle. It is very personal: I don't want to sin. The second lasting response was an eagerness to clear myself, and to keep myself clear. It is again very personal: I want my relationship with God and with people to be right. The third result is indignation. It is personal in the sense that I am angered at temptation and at Satan the tempter. I become angry when I see what Satan has caused on earth: I want to do something about it. Indignation begins to stir me to activity for others as well as for myself. This is not at all surprising, because the very life of Jesus was *lived* for others as well as *sacrificed* for others.

Indignation has an object, as has love or other emotions. It is possible to direct our indignation at the wrong object. For example, I am indignant against Islam. I was studying Islam before I became a believer in Christ, and I understand the ability of Islam to draw, enslave, and eventually destroy people. I have seen what Islam has done to individuals and to nations. Therefore I am indignant against Islam! But I am not indignant against *Muslims*! They are the *victims* of this Satanic deceit. They believe a lie and are merely living as they are taught. I see every Muslim as a potential believer in Christ, a spiritual brother or sister. I know that each year tens of thousands *do* indeed come to Jesus. In my indignation against Islam I aggressively pray against it, and lovingly pray *for* Muslims as individuals and as a group.

Jesus was indignant—at least as I picture Him in certain situations. In Mark 7, the Pharisees and teachers of the law asked Jesus why His disciples did not live according to the traditions of the elders instead of eating with unclean hands. Jesus replied, "Isaiah was right when he prophesied about you hypocrites" (verse 6). That was indignation! In Mark 11 (and other places) when He cleared the temple of merchants and money changers, I think He was quite indignant when He said they had made the temple grounds into a den of robbers. In Matthew 12, He declared that it was a wicked and adulterous generation that sought a miraculous sign. In the incident previously mentioned in Mark 3, when Jesus met the man with the withered hand He challenged those in attendance by asking if it was lawful to do good on the Sabbath. When they would not respond, He was angry and deeply distressed, or I would say indignant! I think Jesus was indignant also when some of those present rebuked the woman who poured perfume on His head (Mark 14) and spoke condemningly about her "waste." His response was quite sharp.

Indignation is active and directed. Having it properly directed may not seem like an important factor, but as we proceed through the characteristics of the result of the changes brought by godly sorrow, we will see these becoming stronger in terms of the emotions and actions they produce. It is important to focus our emotions properly at the beginning—lest, when our emotions have grown more intense, we find ourselves to be destructive rather than redemptive in our actions.

For example, pro-life activists are indignant against abortion. If their indignation is properly focused they can lovingly present their message, keep women from aborting their babies, and hopefully make an impact at the legislative level locally and nationally. When their indignation is *not* properly focused, the result can be hatred and violence: abortion clinics are bombed or burned; doctors are threatened or killed. A good purpose then becomes destructive instead of redemptive, and laws are passed to protect abortionists and their activities. This is a simplistic example, but I hope illustrative.

Christians and the Church as a whole have been victims of indignation since the time of Jesus. The Sanhedrin (Jewish council) was indignant at the teachings of Jesus and moved to eliminate Him. Saul of Tarsus was indignant at what he felt to be a perversion of Judaism, so he moved to eliminate it. He later became a victim of the same kind of indignation. The Roman empire was indignant at what they considered treasonous and atheistic tendencies in Christianity. Regardless of the predominant religion of a country or region of a country, when the gospel is clearly presented, the result is indignation. Yes, there are those who respond and come to Jesus—that is the reason God called us to take His message to all people. However, there is almost always a negative backlash. It is indignation at what is somehow considered unworthy, unjust, or base. Men and women without Christ do not have godly discernment, so they often make improper judgments; and since they do not have the Spirit of Christ, they do not have His restraint.

So what about us? Properly directed indignation and the activism it produces are biblical. This kind of indignation at the deception and destruction generated by paganism helped spread the gospel throughout the Roman Empire within a century. Yes, love was the positive motivation (if I can use that phrase), but in the end, godly indignation at what is unworthy, unjust, and base is truly a manifestation of love. God is love (1 John 4:16)—we know that; He is also a consuming fire (Hebrews 12:29). These two ingredients need likewise to work together in us.

Indignation is not a wimpy word but a strong one, in which action is added to emotion. Indignation brings change! We are now ready to proceed to the next characteristic produced by the transformation begun by godly sorrow. It is a *very* strong word: *Fear*.

Chapter Six

What Fear; What Alarm!

In the previous chapter we looked at indignation. It is a word expressing emotion, activism, and change. In this chapter we look at a word expressing a different idea, one that causes us to reconsider, slow down, change direction and maybe stop. In the various versions that I examined to see what English word was used, I found two words were chosen almost equally: "fear" and "alarm." The New English Bible uses "apprehensive"; the Contemporary English Version says "shocked." I looked at the 16 versions, at commentaries and other helps, and decided to use "fear" as this fourth product of repentance stemming from godly sorrow.

In Chapter Two I spoke about conviction, the knowledge that we have been found guilty. Since Jesus took our guilt, we are offered the opportunity to repent of our sins and to be free from them. Conviction is powerful. It made us want to repent! Fear is powerful too—that is why I want to use it. As

conviction moves us to repentance to escape condemnation, so *fear* moves us to flee temptation to
escape sin and its destructive consequences.

When I was younger I was taught in church that
to "fear God" meant basically to respect Him, be in
awe of Him. I was not supposed to be afraid of God
but amazed at Him. The people of Israel were to
fear God, meaning to worship Him and Him alone.
It included the concept of serving Him too.

I won't argue with that. However, in this verse
it does not say "what fear of *God*" but simply "what
fear." The versions that use the word "alarm" don't
seem to be talking of awe, or worship, or service.
They seem to be talking of something scarier. So
what about fear? What does it mean?

I looked into my Greek New Testament to find
the word used for fear in this verse; it is *phobos.* Then
I looked in my reference books to see what this particular word means. Instead of me giving synonyms,
perhaps an illustration would be useful.

Imagine you are walking along a straight country road at night. There are plenty of stars, but no
moon. You can see the road, but little else; the trees
around you appear as silhouettes. You are heading
toward a farmhouse about a half mile away. There
are lights in the windows and a light in the yard.
Still, since they are so far away, the lights merely
show you that you have a destination—they don't

help you see how to get there. As you continue to walk you sense that there is something keeping pace with you—behind the trees beside the road, off to your right. You quicken your pace! So does the shadow behind the trees. You get the feeling it is moving on all fours and that it is quite large. You look ahead toward the farmhouse. Do you dare run? You look back to the right. The shape emerges from the trees, and in a second is between you and the farmhouse. It turns toward you! It is large! It raises up on its hind legs; lifts it front legs and roars! The little light available reflects off its razor-like claws . . . it's a bear! You feel its breath on your face! You feel—respect, awe, wonder? No way! You feel fear! You feel terror! *This* is the kind of feeling expressed in this verse.

Why would fear be a quality Paul commends to Christians as something positive, and even normative, for someone who wants to live a godly life? Because it is *fear* that keeps us from *sin*.

What about love? If I love God with all my heart and soul and mind, won't I be faithful? Won't I abstain from sin? Won't I live a model life? My response is, "Have you?" Has love adequately motivated you to walk in purity and holiness and complete consistency? Have you kept yourself blameless? Have you consistently been a model of morality in your actions and attitudes? Have you kept every thought under control?

Love *is* a powerful motivation. I wish it was enough to make us walk perfectly before God, but what we see in the lives of many Christians indicates that it is not. It is not that God is not perfect, it is that *we* are not. We are still being perfected in our new nature. Our love is not perfect; our understanding is not perfect; nor is our wisdom or our discernment. In addition, Satan is a powerful *deceiver*. When he can't deceive, he entices. When that fails, he intimidates. He reminds us that we once enjoyed sin, and suggests that a little taste now would not hurt us. Of course, just "a little taste"—we wouldn't want to actually do anything bad!

Go ahead, lose your temper for a bit. You can apologize later if you need to. So what if the sitcom is getting vulgar—it won't really affect you. Cheating on your taxes is not really lying or stealing. Linger a little at the magazine section of the market; you don't plan to buy any of the racy ones, so it's okay. Go ahead and dream a bit of what it would be like to go for a nice dinner with your co-worker who seems to be paying extra attention to you. You are unappreciated at home; all you are wanting is someone who listens to you!

Have these thoughts or others like them come into your head since you believed? From what source have they come? Now look around you: How many people do you know who seemed to be strong Christians but have fallen into major sin? Why did they do it? How *could* they do it? The point is, they did! Their spiritual resources either were not adequate to sustain them against the barrage from the devil, or else they did not know how to appropriate the resources they had. They needed another, *stronger* level of hope or motivation. *Fear* can be this motivation.

Does something strike you as unbiblical about this? After all, as 1 John 4:18 states, "There is no fear in love. But perfect love drives out fear, because fear has to do with punishment. The one who fears is not made perfect in love." So how do love and fear fit together without contradicting the Word of God? One element of the answer is to remember that Paul declares that this fear is a result of the work of God's Spirit in us; and there is no indication that Paul meant this as a passing event—something that would motivate us in one instance and then vanish.

So how *do* these come together? Let's look at *what* we are meant to fear. Are we to fear *judgment*? No! Our guilt has been removed: Jesus took the punishment for our sins. We have been born again. We are a "new creature," or a "new creation" in Christ, depending on the version from which you read 2 Corinthians 5:17.

Do we fear the *devil*? No! Jesus came to *destroy* the works of the devil (1 John 3:8). The Spirit of God now lives within us and the devil has no legal right to any part of us, body, soul or spirit. Yes, he does go about like a roaring lion seeking to devour us (1 Peter 5:8), but he can't. Okay, granted, I'm being simplistic—but accurate. We don't take the devil lightly, but we also don't fear him.

Do we fear *God*? No! Not in the sense in which "fear" is used in our text here. We are in *awe* of Him. We do respect, adore, worship, serve and honor Him, and we give Him every other aspect of adoring fear. But our relationship with Him is based on love—His love with which He first loved us (1 John 4:19), and the love He put into our hearts with which we now love Him.

So what *do* we fear? I suggest that what we should fear is *sin.* No, not the *power* of sin, because if Satan has no right in our lives, sin has *no* power over us. This is the obvious teaching of Romans 6–8. So how or why should we fear what has no power over us? Isn't that simply wrong?

No, we fear sin because we fear the *consequences* of sin! At this point I have no intention of getting into a theological argument that pits the Arminian and Calvinistic positions against each other. So we are not looking at the *eternal* consequences of sin, we are looking at the immediate and long-term results in *this* life. How does sin affect our *lives,* our *ministries,* our *families*? I think we will find no difference in the answers that could be presented by either of the two major theological camps.

First, there are what may be called "little" sins, the ones about which no one else really knows. No, I really don't know how to distinguish between little and big sins, but in terms of the extent of the consequences some may be lesser. These sins may be covetousness, envy, lust, anger, bitterness, resentment, pride, and others that exist only in our hearts and minds. We do not knowingly act on these. Most likely, no one knows if we are struggling with or embracing them.

What if we yield to temptation and let these thoughts continuously live in us? Obviously, they hinder our relationship with God. We cannot go before Him in holiness and joy and worship and praise if we knowingly harbor sinful thoughts and attitudes. He will show us these failings and tell us to get rid of them. If we refuse, we know we have a strained relationship; we cannot really love Him and disobey Him simultaneously. The loss in relationship with our heavenly Father is a dire consequence. Even if this should be the *only* consequence, it is a severe one.

These sinful thoughts and attitudes often hinder our relationships with others. We find it hard to

work with others if we harbor feelings of covetousness or jealousy or pride or lust, or any other ungodly feeling. We find it hard to participate in the
community of the church when the Spirit within us
makes us aware of our hypocrisy. When we pray
with others, we are aware that we are living a lie.
Our fellowship with the body of believers suffers.
This, too, is a severe consequence.

We are clearly aware from Scripture that we
don't have to remain in this condition. We can confess these sins and repent and do what God requires
and be free. The consequences of these sins are rarely
lasting, once we truly deal with them.

Then there are what may be called "bigger" sins,
because the consequences of these may be longer-
lasting and appear more severe. Lying is one of these
because it really affects our relationship with others. Even if we repent and confess, our reputation is
affected. The same with stealing, and many other
sins for which we may get caught. While forgiveness and restoration are urged in 2 Corinthians 2
and Galatians 6, I think we have all seen cases in
which, though restoration to the Christian community is offered and desired, the sin by the believer
has built a barrier that remains. I am not saying this
is right or biblical—just that it happens.

Then there are sins for which the consequences
are devastating and seem to be *very* long-lasting,

perhaps permanent! These may affect those in ministry more than others in terms of career, but the devastation it brings to families is not limited to those in ministry. How many pastors (or missionaries) do we know about who have fallen into sexual sin and had to leave their ministry—the life they had built to that point? These falls have been devastating, and they cross denominational and theological lines. How many Christian families do we know that have been shattered by immorality? Every report I read seems to indicate that more and more Christians are becoming hooked on pornography. Satan is only too happy to help the partner or family of the one involved to discover the "indiscretion." Trust and respect evaporate!

I don't want to prolong this, but could these sins and the consequences have been avoided? The Bible is absolutely clear that the answer is yes. 1 Corinthians 10:13 clearly indicates that no individual sin is stronger than the spiritual resources we have available within us. Romans 8 absolutely reinforces this.

If we can successfully resist and overcome temptation, why don't we? Because we are not *afraid* of sin and its consequences. We dwell on what we feel to be the pleasurable aspects of the thought or act. We don't have enough fear of the result! To those who say that *love* is enough to keep us from sin, I answer that for so many love has *not* been enough! Did they need more love? That seems undeniable. However, if they had a good measure of *fear of sin and the consequences,* that surely would have helped. Again, God is the source of all godly love; He is also the source of all godly fear. If both are from Him, then let's incorporate *both* into our arsenal for overcoming temptation and avoiding sin.

As much as God has enabled me, I dearly love Him. I clearly want to avoid sin. Yet in my own life I have found that in certain temptations I have been greatly helped by remembering the devastation that yielding to a similar temptation has brought on others. I backed away—far and fast! Was Satan helping me think about the consequences? I seriously doubt it. I am confident it was God, or more precisely the Holy Spirit! I was motivated enough to overcome the temptation and to erect barriers to keep myself from similar situations. In talking to many friends, I have found they are doing similar things. Not one of us feels that a good dose of fear at specific times has been an indication of condemnation, but rather was a blessing from God. *We don't live in a state of fear,* but we appreciate it when the Spirit uses it on our behalf.

Once we came to Jesus, we became careful to avoid sin. We wanted to clear away barriers former sins had built between us and others. We became indignant against sin, not wanting to be corrupted in any way. Now, when our *love* for God is not enough of a motivation to overcome temptation, He reminds us to fear the consequences. Since He has made us free moral agents, He probably can't do any more than this to keep us from sin.

One final thought about fear. I am not talking about living in a *state* of fear. I am not even talking about being fearful every time a temptation arises. I am talking about having a sense of fear whenever I am tempted and do not immediately resist and overcome that temptation. If I begin to truly consider doing the sinful act or find myself harboring sinful thoughts, *that* is when I hope for and actually expect the sensation of fear. God's "alarm bell" can be a genuine blessing.

As we look at the next three results of godly sorrow, we'll see a major shift. The first four that we have examined serve primarily to help us maintain a good relationship with God, and to establish and maintain good relationships with people. In other words, they have a lot to do with *me.* The final three also involve me, but they are much more *outwardly* and evangelistically directed. Now that we are walking well with our God, we are ready to be more about our Father's *business*!

Chapter Seven

What Vehement Desire; What Longing!

Of the seven characteristics of a maturing Christian expressed in 2 Corinthians 7:11, this is the one that was initially the most puzzling, especially when I began reading reference books. Interestingly enough, most of them agreed fairly well on what these phrases in the KJV ("what vehement desire") and the NIV ("what longing") meant—for which I was grateful. It just did not "come through" in the text.

The Phillips version and the New English Bible present the idea much more clearly, so I will quote these. "Look how it made you long for my presence" (Phillips); "How your longing for me awoke" (NEB).

What a result! Not only had the Corinthians gained a stronger relationship with God, but now they wanted to see Paul again. He was the one who sent the strong, stinging letter. It hurt! It cut! Yet the Corinthians treated the pain like the pain inflicted by a doctor working to cure a deadly disease. They were grateful to Paul and wanted to see him again.

That's nice, but so what? What does the desire to get back together have to do with Christian maturity? Volumes! (Fortunately, I won't write *that* much.) It shows they really were maturing, and they knew the best way to *continue* the process was to be under the teaching of the most mature and godly teachers they could find. Paul certainly fit that description.

I had such an example in my own life. My mother's mother was a special and wonderful person. I always knew her as Grandma Puckett. Puckett was her married name and therefore my mother's maiden name. Grandma Puckett was born and reared in the mountains of Virginia. She married young and had seven children, six boys and my mother, who was the middle child in the family. (This would be a wonderful time to tell stories about how the first three picked on Mom, so she picked on the younger three. I could also relate how, as they grew up, the older three took their responsibilities as older brothers seriously, to Mom's joy and benefit. However, since a couple of the younger brothers are still living at the time I am writing this,

I had best stick to information I know to be true.)

Although I met Grandma Puckett various times when I was young, I never really got to know her until after she moved in permanently with my parents, sometime following their return from Turkey (Dad was in the Air Force) in late 1969. I was already in college and essentially living on my own, so my time at home was usually measured in days or, at the most, weeks. Still, Grandma Puckett became tremendously important to me.

She was one of the most spiritual people I have ever known. She was not highly educated, nor was she sophisticated by worldly standards. But she knew Jesus intimately. She knew Him so well it was scary. In one sense, it was as if I were visiting with Moses, who had to veil his face after meeting with God because the Israelites could not stand the glory shining from him. Grandma did not really glow, but she radiated Jesus.

I give her a tremendous amount of the credit for my conversion. She prayed for me daily for years until I came to Jesus. Afterwards, she continued to pray for me daily. So when I would go to my parents' home, we would pray together. I loved and hated it. I so much wanted to go with her into her room, where we would kneel by her bed and pray. We were so evidently in the presence of God, I felt I would see Him if I peeked (which I did on occasion); we were kneeling in His holy presence. It was wonderful! Yet while we knelt there I felt as though every evil thought and feeling I ever had was being played on a large screen. I felt so unholy and unworthy! I kept waiting for Grandma to turn and rebuke me. It was terrible!

When we prayed together, I knew I was going to leave ready to take whatever the next step would be in my spiritual growth, even though she never said anything to me about it. She was so humble she felt she knew nothing, although she read her Bible countless times. I could not be around her and *not* grow. The Corinthians must have had a similar experience with Paul.

When he was with them he taught them by the power of the Spirit. He was teaching and they responded! God moved in the city and, of course, in the church. Then when Paul left, carnality entered. Spiritual warfare raged! Carnality and holiness are not the best of companions. No wonder there were divisions in the church.

Then Paul wrote to the church, and we have that recorded as 1 Corinthians. What a scorcher of a letter! But as Paul notes in 2 Corinthians 7, Titus visited Corinth and saw that the church had responded positively to Paul's letter. Paul's dread of the next visit—in which he thought he might have to mete out major discipline—turned to joy at the prospect of fellowship with those as eager to serve God as he was. The Corinthians wanted Paul to visit because they wanted to grow! They wanted the best possible teaching, and they knew Paul could give it because he was part of the founding team of the church in Corinth.

They knew Paul could teach well, and his teaching was confirmed by evidences of the power of God. But his teaching was not the kind that pleased carnal Christians: it cut deeply. Paul was a man ready to die for Jesus and he expected nothing less from anyone who was called a Christian. What he gave was solid spiritual meat for those ready to grow. This made him a *challenging* teacher. When people went to church to hear Paul it was possibly something like, "I don't think I can stand this . . . but I sure want to get it." Maybe it was what someone like me feels if he gets onto a roller coaster or something comparable: "I must be crazy to do this . . . but I can't wait!"

This is how the Corinthians were with Paul. This is how I was with Grandma Puckett! I *longed* to be with her! The rate of my spiritual growth was astounding when we were together.

I suspect I've made this sound introspective—though at the end of the last chapter I said the last three traits will tend to make us more evangelistic and other-people oriented. That was the result of being with Grandma. I was charged up, fueled up, fired up, and prayed up! I was eager to live for Christ, and my actions matched my eagerness.

Grandma Puckett has been dead for a number of years. However, God is faithful to allow me to be confronted and taught by others who make a significant impact on my life—if I am willing. I want to retain this eagerness to be challenged, to be confronted, and by God's grace to see the ongoing transformation in my life as I become more like Jesus. But I have to *want it* to happen! The KJV uses the words "vehement desire" to describe the attitude of the Corinthians. I want that same intensity to describe my desire to be like Jesus, and therefore I want to be around people who will, by their teaching and example, strongly *challenge* me.

Chapter Eight

What Zeal; What Concern!

In Chapter Seven we considered having a vehement desire to be like Jesus. One important step in this is to be taught by those who will challenge us to allow God—and even more to *ask* Him—to make this ongoing change in us, even when it is not pleasant. So, where do we go now?

The next characteristic of a deepening life in Christ is expressed by the words "zeal" and "concern." I continue to be amazed by the way the KJV and the NIV complement each other. Either of these two words would give me an idea of how to live for Jesus. Each, however, is inadequate to express the *full* idea I believe Paul wants to communicate. By using both of these, and looking also at other versions of the same verse, we can, I think, get a fuller and therefore better idea.

The King James Version uses "zeal." What do you think of when you picture a zealous person? I think of someone committed to a cause. Someone willing to make a lot of personal sacrifice for this cause. Someone who will make this cause to be successful if it is at all possible. This person will be on the front lines, leading the charge. He will give his money, his time, and perhaps even his life! In other words, a zealot is one essentially consumed by the cause. It gives him purpose, identity, and perhaps even direction. Zealots have a "mission"!

The New International Version uses "concern." I find this harder to define or describe outside the context of a dictionary. So I look at Jesus. After all, *He* is our ultimate model. In Him I see a zealot with a truly human face. Jesus was characterized by zeal. He quoted the verse, "Zeal for your house will consume me" (John 2:17; Psalm 69:9) and applied it to Himself. He was absolutely committed to seeing the purpose for which He came to earth completed.

If the cause were just to get people to "obey" God, Jesus could have joined the ranks of the Pharisees and given sermons filled with fire and brimstone and judgment, punctuated by miracles to instill the proper level of fear and awe into His hearers. His cause was to bring people to "know" God! This was vastly different. Yes, God is a God of fire and of judgment; He is also—I believe even more so—a God of love and of blessing, a Father who desires to have a very personal relationship with each of us. How could Jesus demonstrate this? By His compassion, His care, His concern.

The Pharisees generally spoke with a sternness that was like an outstretched arm that pushed men to the ground as they became aware of their guilt. Jesus generally spoke with a compassion that was like an outstretched arm extended to lift people from the ground as they became aware of God's grace.

Most of us probably identify more with either zeal or concern—one or the other. I am definitely more the zealous type. My wife, Linda, is more the concerned type. This was evident in our personalities and ministry early in our relationship. I was more concerned with teaching the truth and being sure people responded accordingly. I didn't have much time for those who were slow to respond or who seemed to have difficulties. I would tell people to get up out of sin, and even how to do it, but I did very little to assist them. I was of the personality type that Bill Gothard calls a "prophet." Linda was much more of what Bill Gothard calls a "mercy." Yes, he actually did put it that way in a conference for pastors that he led. Linda would see people in a difficult circumstance and she would care; she would bandage them and minister to them. However, if they were in the situation due to their own actions she might not ever tell them they had sinned or had at least been foolish or disobedient. She would definitely make them *feel* better, but they might not *be* better.

I have exaggerated our differences slightly, but not too much. If people wanted an answer, they came to me. If they wanted an understanding ear, they came to Linda. Which of us was better? Have fun with that one. The point I want to make is that neither of us was complete in the way we ministered. (We have both moved toward the middle in our years of ministry, but we still show some of our distinct personalities.) In the same way, by taking the two words "zeal" and "concern" as two aspects of one expression of a tremendous commitment to serve and honor Jesus, we get a better picture of what Paul was trying to illustrate. In our zeal we will be willing to work in "a rescue shop within a yard of hell" (to quote C.T. Studd), and in our concern we will lovingly embrace the unclean and unholy ones who live at the edge of the pit.

One expression of the combination of zeal and concern is "speaking the truth in love" (Ephesians 4:15). Another is a term we hear in contemporary teaching: "tough love." I would speak the truth, toughly if necessary. Linda would show love. By God's grace, as we seek to be more like Jesus, we are influencing each other, and I believe we are getting closer to how Jesus would have us represent His name.

This chapter has focused on terms like "cause" and "ministry." This is because the godly sorrow that brought us to repentance and to Jesus brought us not only to desire godly relationships with *others*, but to the desire to lead others to *Jesus*. We who love and trust the Savior probably have two reasons for still being on the planet. The first is that the process of *sanctification*—the active working of the Holy Spirit within—might be accomplished in us. The second is that we may be *witnesses* to all mankind of the redemptive ministry of Jesus. The first might be done somewhat privately. The second is very public. It requires zeal *and* concern, two sides of the same coin of this next-to-last characteristic.

Chapter Nine

What Revenge; What Readiness to See Justice Done!

This is the seventh and last characteristic of what, I believe, Paul sets forth as a standard pattern for Christian growth. Yet as I read this passage, I sometimes wish he had excluded this last one. It is a characteristic or quality that is easily misunderstood, and therefore can be misapplied with disastrous results.

Perhaps this is why it is the *last* in the list: It may generally be the last to be attained; although that might make the list sound like an orderly progression in which we complete one and proceed to the next, like completing grades in school. I don't believe it's like that at all—in the sense that once we finish, we move on to the next and never look back. Instead, it is that we *learn* the necessary skills at one stage and are then able to *apply* them in the future. Of course, like in school, we may need "refresher lessons" now and then.

When we looked at the previous characteristic we saw that concern and zeal combine to give a balanced approach to ministering to others. What do you get if you combine *revenge* and *justice*? You get something that sounds harsh, judgmental; something that inflicts pain and punishment; something that may be final and unchangeable. It surely sounds to me like something I would rather leave to God.

There are some things that are easily and even best done by individuals. There are other things that are perhaps carried out best by a group or a committee, or, in legal circles, determined by a jury. Revenge and the administration of justice may fit into that category. Why?

One reason is that I don't mind being a channel of blessing indiscriminately. When Linda and I were involved in church planting in Guinea-Bissau, we were specifically working among the Fula and Mandinka tribes. We were there to see the hold of Islam broken on these peoples. However, in the process there were people from the animistic Balanta, Papel, Manjaco, and other tribes converted also. It was "accidental" from our perspective, but there was certainly no way we could tell them that God did not want them saved. (Two of these converts are now pastors.) Many times, what we do as Christians spreads beyond our immediate target. Therefore I will gladly be involved in administering blessing.

However, I don't like administering justice—for I know my knowledge is limited, my wisdom is imperfect, and that I am certainly not without sin; so I don't want to be involved in casting stones at others. Yet discipline is a part of church life. The discipline administered to Ananias and Sapphira was abrupt and permanent. How could Peter simply pronounce death upon someone who was part of the fledgling church? He did it because he knew it was the will of God, and in reality it was the Holy Spirit who carried out the sentence! Peter did not personally lift a hand against them.

How often am I sure enough to pronounce discipline, even something far less than a sentence of death, upon anyone? By myself, probably never. This is where a group—comprised of the elders or spiritually mature people of a congregation—*together,* are probably the best way to approach such a subject. But *Peter* didn't ask for a committee decision! *Paul* did not ask the church what they thought about the man sleeping with his father's wife (1 Corinthians 5)! Of course, only one of these situations resulted in death.

What happened when Ananias and Sapphira

died? A holy fear came upon the church, and also upon nearby non-Christians, so they were hesitant to casually gather with the believers. What happened with the man in Corinth? 2 Corinthians 7 indicates that he repented; Paul was recommending his restoration. This was *positive*.

It is proper to administer justice in civil society. In fact, it is necessary. The general sinfulness of unregenerate mankind leads only to more sin and *more violent* sin unless there is some kind of authority available to apply force—to ensure conformity. In the church, however, we can say we are surely a body of regenerate people, so the same coercive standard does not need to apply. That's true! Imprisonment and death are not normally punishments meted out by the church in our day. Even so, some kind of sanction has to be available for applying to those who would teach heresies or maintain sinful lives *while calling themselves Christians*.

The early church called for separation from those who were false or sinful brethren. *Who* called for or enforced such separation? Usually it was the leadership of the church. But be wary. Third John shows how such power in the hands of one man can lead to corruption. History also shows that entire groups can become corrupt, so even supervision by several or many does not guarantee biblical standards. An imperfect system, however, does not mean the system should be thrown out entirely. Since fallible men are the ones to administer justice in the church and in society in general, it means we need to be very careful whom we appoint or elect, but it does *not* mean we cease to administer justice.

In our study of the "characteristics of a believer" we have moved from those that are personal—concerned with my own relationship with God and others—and into the characteristics that equip us to engage in ministries on behalf of the church, and now to this final one, the maintenance of the purity of the church itself.

What about biblically sanctioned revenge? The "administration of justice" sounds more appropriate. Where does "revenge" fit in the life of a believer? It must, in some way, since this definitely is the word used! If you refer back to Chapter One you will notice that various translations use different words; you will see "avenging," and that several versions use forms of the word "punish." "Revenge," "avenge," "punish"—these are all strong words, words which we think of as belonging to the domain of God and Jesus when *they* administer judgment. Yet here they are, in the realm of the church and, potentially, individual believers. What does it mean? Upon whom are *we* to apply revenge?

Before I give a very personal example, let me remind you that when Paul is writing to the same church about ungodly actions and attitudes, he says that we shall someday "judge angels" (1 Corinthians 6:3). We certainly don't find a lot of elaboration on this in other passages, but if we are going to do anything of that magnitude later, then perhaps it is right to consider the idea of revenge for the present time.

This illustration is somewhat difficult to give, for two reasons. First, it involves someone I loved and whose memory I still cherish. Secondly, this person, although deceased, is very dear to a number of people who may read this book and who may not feel totally comfortable with my description of her spiritual position. Still, it is the very best illustration I have, so I'll do my best to make the account accurate. I believe it will also bring you joy as you read it.

Before Linda and I married I had the pleasure of meeting her parents on several occasions. I had a special and wonderful relationship with each one. Among many other things we discussed, one topic was their spiritual state. Linda's mother, Velma, was very consistent in attending church. However, when we talked, she told me clearly that she had no assurance that she was "saved" or that she would go to heaven when she died. She believed in heaven and wanted to go there, but she was not sure. She also said she had been saved several times, but it never "stuck."

During one conversation about the Bible she said that while she liked what Jesus said, she did not like what Paul wrote. She chose to believe and to apply *part* of the New Testament, and she chose to reject *other* parts! Linda and I shared with her several times that the Bible is a unit. It is either *all* the inspired Word of God, and we are therefore accountable to believe all of it, or in reality *none* of it is the sure Word of God. She said she would continue to apply the parts of it she liked and leave the rest.

In 1982, after Linda and I had returned to America and were working at the WEC headquarters in Pennsylvania, Linda's mother became ill. It seemed serious, so Linda and our very young son Andrew flew to Ohio to be with her. Becky and I stayed in Pennsylvania, since Becky was in school and we didn't want to pull her out until we knew more.

On the Wednesday morning after Linda left for Ohio, I received a call from her. Her mother was being taken into surgery for what seemed to be a bowel obstruction, when the bowel ruptured, and she died. Since she was literally on the way to surgery, the doctors were able to resuscitate her! However, it became obvious that her condition was very critical. At the time Linda called, our entire WEC staff happened to be in a prayer meeting, so we all began to pray for Linda's mother. I remember sensing a horror and misery at the possibility of her dying without knowing Jesus. The words that came into my mind again and again were "Forever is a long, long time."

After the prayer meeting I got Becky from school and we drove to Ohio. When I went into the Intensive Care Unit, Velma was there, semiconscious, hooked to a number of machines that were sustaining her life and monitoring her vital signs. I took her hand and said something like this: "Velma, you know that Linda and I love you very much. We know what you believe about Jesus and the Bible, because you have told us. You know that we believe that if you die now, you will be lost and will go to hell. We cannot stand that thought. Will you please accept Jesus as your Lord and Savior, as we have explained to you before?" Although at best she appeared merely semiconscious, she gave a very deliberate and clear nod of her head. Though she could not talk, there was a witness in my heart that she definitely received Jesus at that moment. She died a few days later.

I felt two simultaneous emotions. The first was a rush of joy and of gratitude to God for preserving Velma and allowing her to come to know Him. The second was a sense of rage at Satan for having done his best to destroy her and cause her to go to hell. I rejoiced at his defeat and felt he was absolutely miserable over Velma's decision. I believe he is absolutely miserable *every* time someone is truly converted, and even more miserable when they go to be with Jesus! I found myself rejoicing in his misery. This was revenge! The destroyer had his prey taken from him! The roaring lion had no one to devour! Velma was safe with Jesus!

How is it "revenge"? Is it a cop-out to say "because *God* says so"? I know *I* don't really feel or understand exactly what Paul means. I *do* know that every time I witness to someone and they come to Jesus, that is *revenge* because it takes from Satan what he thought he had. Every time I witness to someone, even if they aren't converted then, I may be part of a chain of witnesses that eventually serves to bring that person to Jesus. So that is, in a sense, revenge too. Every time I resist temptation I am defeating Satan. That also is, in a sense, *revenge.* Each person I teach or encourage who resists temptation is *defeating Satan!* That person and I are *both* participating in revenge. Each time I pray for someone, or for a people-group, or for a nation, I am participating in "revenge" because God is answering prayers!

In other words, I don't always have to feel that I am exacting revenge in order for it to be happening. On some occasions, as it was with Velma, or as it was at my mother's funeral when my father told me he had decided to become a Christian, there is a sense of tremendous joy, triumph, worship, and a multitude of other such wonderful words. Jesus has triumphed! Satan has been overcome!

When Jesus opened the fifth seal (Revelation 6:9–11) the saints beneath the altar were asking for revenge. God told them it was coming; they were not rebuked or criticized. They were aware of what God intended, knew it was just, and wondered when it would happen. It is much like the disciples asking Jesus, in Acts 1, if that was the time for the restoration of the kingdom to Israel. They, too, were not rebuked, although their vision was redirected—not to something as small as the kingdom being restored to Israel, but something as large as the Church being established throughout the earth.

How is that supposed to encourage and motivate us? If we realize that every time we share our faith, or pray with faith, or teach someone to grow or respond in faith, we are *actively defeating Satan,* we might be prone to do these things more often. Ought we to be motivated purely by love to serve Jesus? That would certainly be wonderful and honorable. However, remember that in Chapter Six we said it is great to avoid sin because we are motivated by *love,* but God grants us the same result through motivation by *fear.* This was positive, not negative. In various passages Jesus talks about *rewards* for those

who are faithful. Are we to be motivated by reward, or by *love*? Love certainly sounds more noble
or spiritual, but it is Jesus Himself who promised
reward, and He said it in order to *motivate* us! This,
too, is positive, not negative. In the same way,
though it is wonderful to share our faith because
we are motivated chiefly by love, yet it is God who
through Paul includes "revenge" or "conquest" or
"overcoming" as a positive motivation. It is not that
we have pride or confidence in ourselves. We are
capable of *nothing*. Our pride and confidence are
in *Jesus. He* is the Lion of Judah! *He* is the Con-
queror! *He* is the one who has crushed the head of
Satan! We are but part of the host rejoicing in His
victory, in His coming Second Advent, and in His
ultimate glorious reign.

As we grow in our maturity we finally come to
the point of being ready to see *justice* done at a spiritual level. Sometimes we may even be involved in
its administration. We also come to see how the
triumph of Jesus is simultaneously the *defeat of Satan*. We greatly rejoice as revenge comes upon him
who would not only corrupt earth and humanity,
but who desires to ascend to the throne of God and
destroy all that is holy.

Paul *rejoiced* that the church in Corinth was capable of understanding this!

Conclusion

Where have we come with the study of this passage? In the beginning, I said I look at it as one of the key passages for Christian growth. It speaks of "godly sorrow" which leads to "repentance," a key evidence of a true conversion. It is often at this point that the "now what" begins. 2 Corinthians 7:11 contains a seven-part answer.

Are these seven parts *consecutive* or *concurrent*? In other words, do they follow one another or build upon one another? Some of both. In many cases they do tend to follow one another, in the sense that the earlier characteristics in the list often appear first in the life of a Christian. The others appear with maturity, although, I believe, very early in the process of maturity. They should not take years to become evident, but months, weeks, or even days. To some degree this will depend upon the follow-up presented by other Christians. Yet as the latter qualities appear, the earlier ones do not disappear. They become a constant part of the life of the believer. They become permanent fixtures.

There is another passage that is similar in that it too has several aspects. These are listed in a sequential order leading to the highest quality, and yet *all* are to be part of the life of the believer *all* the time.

> His divine power has given us everything we need for life and godliness through our knowledge of him who called us by his own glory and goodness. Through these he has given us his very great and precious promises, so that through them you may participate in the divine nature and escape the corruption in the world caused by evil desires.
>
> For this very reason, make every effort to add to your faith goodness; and to goodness, knowledge; and to knowledge, self-control; and to self-control, perseverance; and to perseverance, godliness; and to godliness, brotherly kindness; and to brotherly kindness, love. For if you possess these qualities in increasing measure, they will keep you from being ineffective and unproductive in the knowledge of our Lord Jesus Christ. (2 Peter 1:3–8, NIV)

These are listed in a progression, one leading to the next with the word "add," not "replace," as the key word. Love is the last of the qualities listed, and yet in 1 John 4:7–12 and in numerous other passages, love is listed as a *primary* evidence of a saving faith. Therefore, although it is here the last and highest listed, it also exists from the beginning. In fact, in the listing of the fruit of the Spirit in Galatians 5:22, love is listed *first*, and may be the root from which all the others spring.

In both passages, 2 Peter 1:3–8 and 2 Corinthians 7:10–11, the evidences of a saving faith show both *progress*, in the sense that these come with maturity, and *speed*, in the sense that they are given as standards by which we can measure ourselves. Let's summarize the Corinthian passage one more time:

Godly sorrow—the conviction brought by the Holy Spirit—leads us to repentance that leads to salvation: new birth. Then we begin to grow.

First, we find we are careful in how we act and think, because we do not want to bring shame upon the name of Jesus, and we don't want to hurt our personal relationship with Him.

Second, we want to have a right relationship with others, so we seek to clear away offenses and make restitution.

Third, as temptations come our way, we don't just react calmly and in an almost indifferent attitude resist them. Becoming indignant at the tempter, we resist in this new attitude, growing stronger instead of weaker. What Satan intended as a stumbling block becomes for us a stepping stone.

Fourth, as we mature in our walk, temptations

continue. We know that yielding to certain temptations will be devastating and thus we find we have
a healthy fear that motivates us not to sin. This fear
of sin is coupled with an increasing love for our Lord.

Then we find the fifth quality—a deep longing
for fellowship with mature believers—becoming evident in our lives. We want to be around those who
will motivate us to grow in our faith. These are not
just people who may be pleasant to hear: no, those
who help us the most may also challenge us the most,
and at times will cause us considerable consterna-
tion as we face ourselves. But it is worth it!

Sixth, we find our zeal for the Lord growing. We
are becoming more intense in our desire to serve
Him. This is zeal of the Spirit, a concern that will
hopefully be coupled with wisdom and love, characteristics that will draw someone to the Savior
whom they see reflected in us.

Finally, we are able and therefore ready to be
involved in administering justice. We are not "perfect," but mature. As we do this, we are taking from
Satan what he thinks is his. We see, in a sense, the
beginning of God's revenge upon Satan. We can
hate Satan with a holy hatred, because we love mankind with a holy love!

This hatred for Satan is not transferred to human beings. Peter was told in Matthew 16:19 that
he would be given the keys of the kingdom of

heaven—that whatever he bound on earth would be bound in heaven and that whatever he loosed on earth would be loosed in heaven. What a wonderfully horrible gift and responsibility! We, too, are arriving at this point of maturity in which we have power and authority given by the Spirit of God for the service and glory of God and His Son.

Yes, it is true that godly sorrow *works*! Keep these seven qualities of a transformed life in your heart and mind, and ask God to give you increasing understanding of each.

Finally, in the Introduction I mentioned that I would list a number of other verses which I treasure. As I grow in the Lord, I often use these as reminders. A lot of these passages were submitted by many of the 69 who responded to my questionnaire. (I'm not at all surprised.) I could give you 100, but I'll limit it to 20, counting 2 Peter 1:3–8, which is mentioned above. Please, don't ever ask me to reproduce this list from memory; I would probably get about ten and substitute ten more, because the Bible is full of such wonderful verses and passages. Why don't you make your *own list* of 20 favorites? (I'm going to use the NIV for this list.)

2 Corinthians 5:17: *Therefore, if anyone is in Christ, he is a new creation; the old has gone, the new has come!*—I am not merely redeemed, I am remade.

2 Corinthians 5:21: *God made him who had no sin to be sin for us, so that in him we might become the righteousness of God.*—It expresses the depth of what Jesus became for us and what He really did in us.

Psalm 119:140: *Your promises have been thoroughly tested, and your servant loves them.*—My entire life is based upon God's faithfulness.

Psalm 119:32: *I run in the path of your commands, for you have set my heart free.*—As I fulfill the commandments of the Scripture, I find true freedom and immeasurable joy.

Psalm 119:11: *I have hidden your word in my heart that I might not sin against you.*—I cannot think of anything to add to this obvious truth.

Romans 8:29: *For those God foreknew he also predestined to be conformed to the likeness of his Son, that he might be the firstborn among many brothers.*— There is debate over the doctrine of predestination in terms of conversion and perseverance; I don't think there is any debate over this wonderful verse as applying to Christian growth.

Romans 6:11: *In the same way, count yourselves dead to sin but alive to God in Christ Jesus.*—Now that I am born again, Satan never has any authority in my life, ever. I am dead to him and his power, and absolutely alive in and to Christ.

Romans 5:1–8: *Therefore, since we have been jus-tified through faith, we have peace with God through our Lord Jesus Christ, through whom we have gained access by faith into this grace in which we now stand. And we rejoice in the hope of the glory of God. Not only so, but we also rejoice in our sufferings, because we know that suffering produces perseverance; perse-verance, character; and character, hope. And hope does not disappoint us, because God has poured out his love into our hearts by the Holy Spirit, whom he has given us.*

You see, at just the right time, when we were still powerless, Christ died for the ungodly. Very rarely will anyone die for a righteous man, though for a good man someone might possibly dare to die. But God demon-strates his own love for us in this: While we were still sinners, Christ died for us.—Analyzing this would take another book. Just read slowly through each phrase, and make it personal for yourself.

Ephesians 2:4–10: *But because of his great love for us, God, who is rich in mercy, made us alive with Christ even when we were dead in transgressions—it is by grace you have been saved. And God raised us up with Christ and seated us with him in the heavenly realms in Christ Jesus, in order that in the coming ages he might show the incomparable riches of this grace, expressed in his kindness to us in Christ Jesus. For it is by grace you have been saved through faith—and this is not from yourselves, it is the gift of God—not by works, so that no one can boast. For we are God's workmanship, created in Christ Jesus to do good works, which God prepared in advance for us to do.*—This talks of our past state and our present state. It tells us how we came to be where we are, and what God would have us be and do now.

Ephesians 3:14–21: *For this reason I kneel before the Father, from whom his whole family in heaven and on earth derives its name. I pray that out of his glorious riches he may strengthen you with power through the Spirit in your inner being, so that Christ may dwell in your hearts through faith. And I pray that you, being rooted and established in love, may have power, together with all the saints, to grasp how wide and long and high and deep is the love of Christ, and to know this love that surpasses knowledge—that you may be filled to the measure of all the fullness of God.*

Now to him who is able to do immeasurably more than all we ask or imagine, according to his power that is at work within us, to him be glory in the church and in Christ Jesus throughout all generations for ever and ever! Amen.—This is Paul's prayer for the believers in Ephesus and, I believe, God's intention for His people everywhere.

Ephesians 4:22–24: *You were taught, with regard*

to your former way of life, to put off your old self, which is being corrupted by its deceitful desires; and to be made new in the attitude of your minds; and to put on the new self, created to be like God in true righteousness and holiness.—God has high expectations for me, and has therefore given all that is necessary for this to happen! I will cooperate.

Philippians 1:4–6, 9–11: *In all my prayers for all of you, I always pray with joy because of your partnership in the gospel from the first day until now, being confident of this, that he who began a good work in you will carry it on to completion until the day of Christ Jesus. . . . And this is my prayer: that your love may abound more and more in knowledge and depth of insight, so that you may be able to discern what is best and may be pure and blameless until the day of Christ, filled with the fruit of righteousness that comes through Jesus Christ—to the glory and praise of God.*—This is how I want to live until Christ comes, and God will enable me to do it!

Philippians 2:12–13: *Therefore, my dear friends, as you have always obeyed—not only in my presence, but now much more in my absence—continue to work out your salvation with fear and trembling, for it is God who works in you to will and to act according to his good purpose.*—It is God, not me, so I can do what He expects.

Philippians 3:10: *I want to know Christ and the power of his resurrection and the fellowship of sharing in his sufferings, becoming like him in his death, and so somehow to attain to the resurrection from the dead.*—I want to love Jesus this much.

Philippians 4:4–8: *Rejoice in the Lord always. I will say it again: Rejoice! Let your gentleness be evident to all. The Lord is near. Do not be anxious about anything, but in everything, by prayer and petition, with thanksgiving, present your requests to God. And the peace of God, which transcends all understanding, will guard your hearts and your minds in Christ Jesus.*

Finally, brothers, whatever is true, whatever is noble, whatever is right, whatever is pure, whatever is lovely, whatever is admirable—if anything is excellent or praiseworthy—think about such things.—Much of our Christian walk is based on our attitudes and thoughts. Here are the attitudes and thoughts I want.

2 Timothy 1:7: *For God did not give us a spirit of timidity, but a spirit of power, of love, and of self-discipline.*—If this is what I have, this is how I want to be.

Hebrews 2:14–15: *Since the children have flesh and blood, he too shared in their humanity so that by his death he might destroy him who holds the power of death—that is, the devil—and free those who all their lives were held in slavery by their fear of death.*—I am fully free through Jesus!

1 Peter 4:8: *Above all, love each other deeply, because love covers over a multitude of sins.*—If this is what is "above all," I want to do it. God, help me; because what is above all seems to be hardest of all.

Revelation 19:6b: *Hallelujah! For our Lord God Almighty reigns.*—That says it all!

May you love the Scriptures God has given us! All His words are true, and they are *all* the truth God has given us. May you enjoy the fullness of His Spirit who enables us to understand the Scriptures, and who, because He now lives in us, enables us to live the life the Father has set before us! May you love the Lord your God with all your heart and soul and mind and strength. May you live extravagantly for Jesus, our Brother and our High Priest who gave His life for us and now lives and intercedes for us, and who is preparing our everlasting home. Amen.

Permission to Quote Various Versions:

This book was produced by CLC Publications. We hope it has been helpful to you in living the Christian life. CLC is a literature mission with ministry in over 50 countries worldwide. If you would like to know more about us, or are interested in opportunities to serve with a faith mission, we invite you to write to:

CLC Publications
P.O. Box 1449
Fort Washington, PA 19034

For more information about
WEC International, please contact:

WEC International
P.O. Box 1707
Fort Washington, PA 19034
www.wec-int.org

From the Introduction:

Is there some kind of yardstick, barometer or thermometer to register growth and vitality? In my search through the Scripture, I have found one commonly-neglected passage in Second Corinthians to be surprisingly helpful. It peratains to "godly sorrow" and its effects. May we examine it together?

For over thirty years I have been involved in ministry—as a pastor, a missionary in West Africa, and now a missionary "mobilizer" for WEC International. Like most Christians, I have had questions about God's will concerning my life in terms of career, marriage, actions, attitudes and other things. So I am writing this book as a seeker who has found something that may be useful to other seekers.

Evaluating one's personal spiritual life and growth, that is the topic of this book.

> "If you have a hunger in your heart to know God more intimately and to experience His grace more fully, you will find the wisdom here to be practical, penetrating and perceptive. It was good for me to read it, and it will be good for you too."
>
> *Dennis Kinlaw, Chancellor, Asbury College*